STRATEGIC INQUIRY

Starting Small for Big Results in Education

Nell Scharff Panero
and Joan E. Talbert

Harvard Education Press
Cambridge, Massachusetts

Library of Congress Control Number 2013939173

Paperback ISBN 978-1-61250-584-8
Library Edition ISBN 978-1-61250-585-5

Published by Harvard Education Press,
an imprint of the Harvard Education Publishing Group

Harvard Education Press
8 Story Street
Cambridge, MA 02138

Cover Design and Illustration: Ciano Design
Cover Photo: Yagi Studio/Digital Vision/Getty Images

The typefaces used in this book are Adobe Garamond Pro and Futura.

For Doug

and

for David

Contents

Foreword

Strategic Inquiry is a wonderful book that combines specific change processes with school and system improvement and ends up giving a clear picture of how change can be customized and accomplished. Rarely do we see in high school reform such instructional precision.

First, the model is elegantly simple and comprehensive. It contains four Ts as its foundation: teams, targets, tasks, and training. Within the *tasks* element there are three core change goals, namely the movement of students, systems, and colleagues.

The book is about showing how these Ts work in a particular school. The strength of *Strategic Inquiry* is its specificity, precision, and clarity in laying out what has to happen for real improvement to occur. Here we see the pinpointing of specific skills needed by each student and the instructional responses suited to each set of needs. The causal sequence of the learning process is very clearly captured, as is the impact on student learning outcomes.

A second contribution is that Panero and Talbert show very specifically how teachers change their beliefs. One of the core assumptions of their theory of action is that learning, not teaching, needs to be the primary focus. In other words, the only thing that counts is whether specific students learn specific skills. With great clarity, the authors show that teachers literally change their assumptions and beliefs as a result of learning better instruction geared to the actual needs of the students in question. Here we see the centrality of instructional efficacy as the game changer. They offer some great insights: how precise language must replace vague jargon when it comes to instruction; what up-close diagnosis looks like; and, my personal favorite, how teachers become better consumers of professional development because they know what they are looking for.

Third, Panero and Talbert are equally detailed and clear about the role of support—indeed, the necessity of trained facilitators and of district expectations and processes. They are especially impressive in capturing the subtlety of change leaders insisting on quality processes without imposing them. Trained facilitators, for example, do not accept that some struggling students cannot learn; it has to be all the students. Leadership, to take another example, is not left to a few but requires all colleagues to be involved, including the constant attention to cultivating a pipeline of new leaders.

Any book that can demonstrate that high schools can significantly improve by "moving" previously hard-to-reach students and, I would say, previously hard-to-reach colleagues is a must-read. Panero and Talbert show not only that reaching all students can be done but also how it can be done in a direct applied fashion.

Strategic Inquiry is a gem of convincing clarity. Read it and use the ideas in your own setting. Success will be the reward.

Michael Fullan
Professor Emeritus
Ontario Institute for Studies in Education, University of Toronto

Introduction

In recent decades there has been an endless parade of strategies for improving K–12 education in the United States. Vouchers, charter schools, accountability, value-added teacher evaluations, merit pay, core curriculum . . . the list goes on. Presidential candidates, corporate executives, journalists, governors, members of Congress, academics, parents, policy analysts, diplomats, bartenders—everyone has a solution to the problem of K–12 education. Yet these solutions, popular and unpopular, have failed to improve the heart of teaching and learning largely because they are grounded in faulty assumptions about the underlying problems of change. Either they assume a lack of effort, motivation, or ability among educators and therefore that additional accountability and/or incentives for individuals will push or pull schools to improve, though available evidence indicates otherwise, or they assume that if held to the fire or given sufficient monetary rewards, educators on their own can figure out what it takes to close existing achievement gaps.

What's missing in this picture, and what we aim to present in this book, is a view of educators as intelligent, hard working, and devoted but as going against the grain of schooling in the United States when they try to bring about what the field increasingly agrees is necessary to continuously improve student achievement: collective, evidence-based learning and decision making. Educators struggle against a culture of individualism, tradition-based practice, and "star" leadership. Given prevailing cultural norms, which are more often than not reinforced by the reform efforts that seek to change them, educators cannot make the needed shifts without a structured, tightly designed process to support and guide them. The cultural impediments are too great.

Never has the need for collaborative, evidence-based learning been greater or more likely to yield tremendous rewards in student learning. With the rollout of the Common Core State Standards (CCSS) and related assessments in 2014, U.S. districts and schools are pressed and ready to focus on developing their capacity to meet standards for higher-order student learning. Success will depend, however, on their teachers' ability to close larger-than-ever gaps between students' knowledge and skills and the state standards, and doing so will require a significant shift in teaching culture. In conventional teaching culture, teachers respond to higher standards by creating more rigorous assignments that leave struggling students further behind. Schools in which teams have learned to use state standards and assessments to identify and close student performance gaps—those with an established instructional culture of collaboration and evidence use—are ready to respond to the new CCSS so that struggling students don't fall further behind.

Despite the growing appetite for and efforts to create collaborative, evidence-based decision making in schools, there is little understanding of how to do so consistently or at scale. Currently there are some good models to guide a teacher team in using assessment data to evaluate instruction and address student learning needs in an ongoing cycle, such as the DuFour PLC (professional learning community) model. Many districts across the nation have bought into a PLC approach to instructional improvement, at least nominally; yet few successfully implement it. In large part, the models they use lack guidelines that are structured enough to push against existing cultural forces, lead teachers to bring about systemic change, and develop teacher-leaders as agents of change in support of student learning.

This book features a model for collaborative evidence-based school improvement that does just that. The model is not a silver bullet for education reform. Rather, it is a set of principles and guidelines for developing team leadership to strategically target and eliminate the school conditions that inhibit student success. It is based on evidence of school conditions that are essential to improving student achievement and provides a road map for getting there. It has a track record of improving student performance by changing school culture that is especially strong in large high schools, which have proven notoriously difficult to reform. In the upcoming chapters we illustrate how the model works in diverse school contexts, point to some of the predictable developmental hurdles that school change entails, and describe strategies that have worked to overcome them. We believe that what we present here must be in place for any national reform movement to be successful in the long run.

The strategic inquiry model and lessons featured in this book derive from practice and research in the Scaffolded Apprenticeship Model (SAM) program of school improvement through leadership development. SAM was launched in 2005 as an innovative school leadership preparation program jointly created and run by the School of Public Affairs at Baruch College and New Visions for Public Schools, in which the "applicant" was a team in a New York City high school and the coursework was designed as site-based improvement. The program name refers to its design and goal at that time: an apprenticeship for teacher teams within a school to develop a pipeline of leaders skilled in inquiry-based approaches to school improvement. Since 2005 the SAM leadership certification program has grown beyond high schools to include teams and individuals from all K–12 levels, while its underlying model of inquiry-driven, site-based improvement has been adapted to district and/or school turnaround reform efforts in Oakland, Boston, Rochester and, most notably, in New York City in the form of Collaborative Inquiry, a pillar of the Children First intensive reform, in which every teacher was expected to participate in collaborative inquiry.[1]

We call the model *strategic inquiry* to distinguish it from other designs for inquiry and more generic notions of data-driven decision making or collaborative inquiry. The model is strategic because it is grounded in specific ideas and evidence about what gets in the way of student success, what makes change so hard in schools, what shifts in teacher beliefs and school culture are needed, and what designs for inquiry and leadership development best target and facilitate these shifts. Chief among the model's refinements that have emerged over time is the principle of starting small to make a big difference—the strategy that is most counterintuitive yet most essential to bringing about the desired changes.

In strategic inquiry, teams study the school in microcosm, assuming that a part represents the whole. They identify an essential skill gap for a group of struggling students, investigate how schoolwide learning conditions allow this gap to persist, and design and implement a strategic system change, the effectiveness of which is measured by the closing of the gap. Getting small is essential in the model's theory of change. It makes the otherwise overwhelming task of change manageable, scaffolds and ensures the development of new skills and experiences that shift team members' thinking, and defines a direct line between action and results so that actions can be continually improved and results ensured.

Strategic inquiry works in three ways to improve schools. First, it leads teams to improve outcomes for specific struggling students. These outcomes in and of themselves make a difference, as does the attention paid to specific struggling students who report feeling cared about and attended to and whose skill needs are directly addressed. As a result, the target students often improve in areas beyond those directly studied. Second, it leads teams to improve decision making in systems that serve these and other students, such as aligning decisions about what students are taught (the curriculum) with evidence of student learning needs. This change, in turn, improves decision making in other instructional systems, such as teacher assignment. Third, it extends evidence-based practice, shared accountability, and collective leadership for change across a school by growing the number of people who learn and apply the principles and practices of strategic inquiry.

What we focus on primarily in this book is how the model brings about change through three strategic inquiry phases that share underlying principles for inquiry and interact in a theory of action for school improvement. We touch on but do not address in-depth the findings of hundreds of strategic inquiry teams over the decade since the model's inception, the patterns in what strategic inquiry teams have discovered about student skill gaps and what works to close them. Although not the focus of this book, the findings have implications for school reform efforts writ large.

Strategic inquiry teams repeatedly found that struggling high school students have fundamental skill gaps; and if these gaps are closed, student learning across subjects can be accelerated. In literacy, struggling students often lack skills in linking ideas with appropriate conjunctions, identifying key words and phrases, distinguishing more from less relevant information, and note taking. In secondary mathematics, skill gaps center on fractions, operations with signed numbers, graphs, and literacy skills such as following multiple steps, determining which words are important in word problems, translating key words to mathematical symbols, explaining answers, and sequencing transitions. Team after team has discovered that they cannot make assumptions about what struggling students know and do not know. They have discovered that students not knowing these skills is a result of their not being taught (as opposed to students being unable to learn them), and that when teachers teach these skills, students become engaged, learn, and make giant leaps in their progress. The biggest finding from the teams' evidence-based practice, then, is that what's needed most is improvement in *what exactly* is taught to students and, specifically, that what is taught must include explicit, systematic instruction in foundational skills along with, and to reinforce, core content.[2]

Our book shows the process these teams went through to make these discoveries and what they did to improve student achievement. It has three parts. In Part I we describe strategic inquiry, setting the stage for detailed examples of how it works. Chapter 1 describes the model in terms of its theory of change, core principles, and design elements, all of which have been tested and refined across cities and diverse school contexts. It highlights the *4Ts* of the design for strategic inquiry: teams (teacher collaboration), targets (evidence-use to focus and measure improvement), tasks (three phases of inquiry to bring about school change), and training (facilitators prepared to guide each phase). Chapter 2 provides evidence that strategic inquiry improves student outcomes and that it shifts schools toward an evidence-based culture. We describe the developmental trajectories of change that the model brings about for individuals in a team and for a school. In each case we identify typical beliefs and norms that must change to develop school capacity for continuous improvement.

Part II, the book's core, is an in-depth look at the three phases of strategic inquiry in action in real schools—moving students, moving the system, and moving colleagues. Chapter 3 shows what it looks like when a teacher team uses the model to move struggling students ahead by responding to a particular skill gap identified through inquiry. Chapter 4 illustrates how a team uses the model to move the system by identifying a specific pattern in school decision making that inhibits students from learning the particular skill addressed in the first inquiry phase. Chapter 5 shows how teams bring about school culture change by leading colleagues to learn and apply strategic inquiry. We begin with an in-depth look at how one NYC high school used strategic inquiry to realize steady improvement in student outcomes and then point to other successful approaches to implementing the model, and to specific ways in which schools fall short of enduring culture change. Each chapter in this section highlights the developmentally predictable hurdles that teams encounter, how the model's design elements specifically target and support movement through these challenges, and the facilitator actions that make a difference.

Part III takes up the question of how and whether larger educational systems can bring strategic inquiry to scale. Chapter 6 focuses on leveraging and supporting change in K–12 school districts. Drawing on evidence from research on districts known for their continuous improvement of student achievement, we describe ways in which a district can act to bring inquiry-based improvement to scale. Chapter 7 considers the role of higher education—specifically, how an administrator credentialing program can help to develop schools' capacity for evidence-based improvement. We take the SAM program as a case and describe how it works to develop school leaders for strategic inquiry and what it takes to develop skilled facilitators in the model.

As a designer and leader of strategic inquiry in New York City for nearly a decade (Panero) and a researcher of the model for six years (Talbert), we have determined that its power to transform schools lies not in replication but in adaptation with fidelity to its principles. The core design features can be applied flexibly to schools and districts in diverse state and local contexts. We emphasize the importance of developing facilitators, inside or outside a school, who deeply understand the driving principles so that they can hold tightly to what matters most while loosening their hold on those aspects that must respond to the demands of context. A facilitator plays a key role in leveraging and supporting a school's shift toward an inquiry culture.

Our collaboration on this book is grounded in dialogue over the years to critique and make sense of strategic inquiry, learning from each other as practice informed research and research informed practice. Although our professional careers traveled different routes and brought different knowledge and sensibilities to our investigation, we converge in our view that strategic inquiry is key to improving public education in the United States. We join forces in bringing evidence from practice and research to bear on the promise and prospect of inquiry-based school reform.

PART I

VISION, MODEL, AND OUTCOMES

The call for teachers to work collaboratively and to use evidence to meet the learning needs of all students caught hold during the No Child Left Behind (NCLB) era, when schools were pressed to bring all students to standard, and grew in anticipation of the Common Core State Standards, which raise the bar for student achievement. Although the idea of school as the "center of inquiry" traces back to the early twentieth century, various initiatives to develop collaborative, evidence-based practice in schools have not, by and large, gained traction nationwide.[1] And even where they did—such as with the generously funded Annenberg Challenge Initiative in several major urban centers—they have not fulfilled their promise.[2] This is because the school reform models have been general and not designed to strategically target impediments to change.[3] Changing school culture is more difficult than the initiatives anticipated. Merely asking teachers to work collaboratively and use student data to improve instruction is not enough; rather, the design must engage the particular cultural mind-sets and routines that inhibit change.

In this book we put forth a model—strategic inquiry—that has demonstrated success because it targets specific shortcomings of previous initiatives. In particular, it takes on the prior lack of a well-specified design for inquiry and weak investment in training facilitators to guide the work. For one, strategic inquiry marries school improvement and leadership development. The track record of New York City schools that implemented the model for several years shows significant growth in teachers' leadership and evidence-based decision making, along with steady gains in student achievement. Further, strategic inquiry prepares schools to excel in a policy context that measures success against student learning standards and is raising the bar through the CCSS. Teacher teams trained in strategic inquiry routinely use learning standards to diagnose specific student skill gaps and to help their struggling students meet increased demands for performance.

Strategic inquiry is a design for inquiry-based school improvement that was developed and refined over four trials involving roughly three hundred teachers in more than fifty schools. Refinements focus on just those elements of school culture and practice that are resistant to change. The model is comprised of a highly structured set of tasks along with design features that directly target the challenges involved in re-culturing schools. What's especially hard to change is that schools are places where people work privately and are individually accountable, where past practice and intuition rule over evidence, and where leadership is vested in formal authority or a star rather than shared. The goal of collaborative inquiry of any type, and the strategic inquiry model in particular, is to bring about shifts in school culture toward shared accountability, evidence-based practice, and broad-based leadership.

In this section we detail the elements of the model and show how they work together in an overall theory of school change and present evidence that strategic inquiry brings about desired culture shifts along with improved student outcomes and leadership capacity for continuous improvement. This overview sets the stage for an up-close look at strategic inquiry in action in Part II.

CHAPTER 1

How Strategic Inquiry Works

When New Dorp High School, a large comprehensive high school in Staten Island, started strategic inquiry in 2006, its 55 percent graduation rate and mounting accountability pressure had created a sense of urgency among school leaders. Working with a trained facilitator, eight teams of teacher-leaders and administrators from newly formed interdisciplinary units embarked on a journey to learn and lead inquiry-based school improvement.

In keeping with the "starting small" principle of strategic inquiry, each team used data to select a small group of struggling students and then used fine-grained performance data to identify a specific skill gap that, if addressed, would yield big improvement. One team, focused on the students' Global History State Regents exam results, discovered that most had missed several questions involving graphs. When team members then examined math, science, and social studies course content, they discovered that no course in the school systematically taught graph reading, since that was assumed to be middle school curriculum. The team figured that if it broke down and taught the components of this learning target, the students would make big gains on this high-stakes test.

The team was right. Most of the students passed a mock Global Regents exam, and all had big gains over prior scores. The focus on graphing paid off on math and science performance as well. Armed with evidence, team members approached their colleagues and convinced them that graphing skills should be assessed early in ninth grade and taught directly to students with this skill gap. This and ongoing inquiry cycles demonstrated that struggling students can be successful and attracted more teachers to learning strategic inquiry.

By 2009 it was common practice for every New Dorp teacher to be part of an inquiry-driven learning team and for administrators across key units to make system-level decisions in response to the learning of these teams. By 2012 New Dorp's inquiry engine was developed and refined to such an extent that their graduation rate soared to 78 percent and continues to rise.

Strategic inquiry works to improve student achievement by addressing the learning needs of struggling students at the same time that it develops leadership for inquiry-based reform. It works strategically to leverage and support the development of a school's capacity for continuous improvement.

This approach is successful for three main reasons. First, it takes a developmental approach to school change, starting with a cadre of teachers who become skilled in using the model and then in leading colleagues to do the same. Second, its design for team inquiry leverages the key shifts in teachers' thinking, practice, and school norms necessary for continual improvement. Third, it invests in training facilitators to coach teacher teams and schools through critical junctures in the change process.

Grounded in a theory of change, strategic inquiry makes assumptions about *what* needs to change to improve student success and *how* change comes about through inquiry. Its design for team inquiry is strategic in bringing about shifts in a school's culture to shared accountability, evidence-based practice, and distributed leadership, each of which contributes to a school's ability to continuously improve student performance.

THEORY OF CHANGE AND DESIGN

Strategic inquiry assumes, first, that every school has a sphere of success, a group of students for whom current practices are working, and that every school has limits to that success, students for whom these same practices are consistently not working. It also assumes that practices which limit student success are shaped by school structures, decision rules, and, fundamentally, by beliefs that reflect and maintain the status quo. It further assumes that if school leaders and teachers can come to understand how decision systems in the school work to reliably produce current results—not only for successful students but, more importantly, for those who are not successful—then they will be able to identify and implement strategic changes to improve results.

In essence, the theory of strategic inquiry is that when a teacher team systematically studies the school through the lens of struggling students, it comes to see and then be able to remove obstacles to the students' success. Once team members understand, for example, that a school's curriculum does not address students' specific learning needs, they are then collectively armed—with common understanding and new inquiry and leadership skills—to make and evaluate changes that continuously improve the curriculum and thus student achievement.

Strategic inquiry is designed to bring about the new perspectives and actions that enable teachers and school administrators to respond effectively to student learning needs. It features teacher collaboration and shared responsibility for results, clear targets, inquiry tasks, and trained facilitators to keep teams on track and moving past the roadblocks that can stymie the learning of these skills and practices and school progress. We refer to these design features as the 4Ts: teams, targets, tasks, and training.

Guiding the design for strategic inquiry is the core principle of *getting small to get big results*. This principle emerged through lessons from several iterations of the SAM leader certification program's work with high school teams. The difficulty school teams initially had in accurately diagnosing (and thus responding effectively to) specific student learning gaps led to the discovery that "getting small" was what made it possible for a team to identify and target where, exactly, learning was breaking down for struggling students. This finding was replicated in all subsequent iterations of the program. Getting small was the hardest yet most critical inquiry strategy. Inquiry without first getting small failed to pinpoint what, specifically, target students needed to learn or how instruction in that precise skill brings about improvement. Getting small, therefore, is the critical ingredient in changing teachers' beliefs about the reasons for struggling students' failure and their own efficacy in moving them forward.

Team members' (and other critics') typical, initial insistence that getting small can never yield the rate or scope of needed improvements led the designers of strategic inquiry to clarify the meaning and implications of the principle of getting small to get big results. First, it must be understood as a strategic problem-solving strategy. A team should get small only when it is truly stuck; otherwise it's not worth the time it takes to do so. Second, once new learning has occurred by getting small, a team needs to apply what it's learned to a bigger, more systemic response. In other words, getting small is not an end in itself but a strategy for diagnosing flaws in the larger system so that it can be improved.

Likewise, each of the 4Ts—teams, targets, tasks, and training—is rooted in evidence of its important role in moving schools through what we have come to see as developmentally predictable challenges for inquiry-based reform. Together they stimulate shared accountability, evidence-based practice, and distributed leadership for change.

WHY TEAMS?

Teacher collaboration on school-based teams is fundamental to strategic inquiry for three main reasons. First, the challenges on the table are formidable; current knowledge and practice have led to outcomes that have proven very difficult to change. The collective wisdom of school teams is needed to better understand problems with the status quo and to create new knowledge to solve them. Another way of saying this is that the challenges facing schools require adaptive rather than technical solutions, or for teams to conceptualize them as complex dilemmas to be managed rather than as problems that can be solved. Strategic inquiry assumes that teams, under certain conditions, are better and smarter at addressing challenges than any one individual can be. The complexity of managing current school dilemmas requires this collective wisdom and is worth the time and effort it takes to develop team members' skills and to cultivate the culture of a high-functioning team.[1]

Second, the team creates a practice space within which educators can develop new inquiry behaviors and skills. They begin to forge a new culture within their team that they can later bring to their school. They practice, for instance, the habits of exposing what they do not know and learning with others in public. They do this first in the relatively protected, shared practice space of their inquiry team, which then supports and bolsters them when they spread this culture outward. Simply put, team members need the support of others with whom they have built new practices and ways of thinking to help sustain them when they become immersed in the larger school culture they're working to change.

Third, establishing from the start a team that is collectively responsible for improving outcomes for a specific shared group of students in the school engenders shared accountability. At New Dorp, for example, the team inquiry process helped forge a collective focus on shared students when the school transformed from a large comprehensive high school into smaller learning communities (SLCs). One inquiry team comprised of the new SLC leaders (assistant principal, guidance counselor, math teacher, and social studies teacher) focused on moving ten struggling students in the math teacher's class. Dara Lapkin, the math teacher, was the only team member who taught those ten students at the time. At first the team thought it was a problem that one teacher was primarily responsible for the teaching that would move or not move these students *and* that other team members lacked the mathematics expertise they assumed was essential to help her. Gradually, however, all team members came to see that having members of a team who are not expert in the focal subject is important: they can ask fundamental questions that content specialists wouldn't ask and ensure that the basic mathematics and its component parts are explained clearly enough to students that nothing is overlooked or assumed. As they collectively scrutinized the mathematics and evidence of teaching and learning, they gradually came to own these students as a team. All team members came to understand exactly what the students needed, to actively support the math teacher in providing it, and to implement systems to be applied in their SLC (and schoolwide) in response to what they had learned. Their collective work improved outcomes for the targeted students (and more) and bound them through a focus on "their" students and each other as critical for their own learning, culture shifts needed for the smaller learning community to thrive.

The original team design for large high schools called for multiple teams of six to eight teachers and/or administrators who represented a broad array of units (e.g., subject departments, SLCs, or grade levels). This was strategic for developing inquiry leadership that would reach across the school and become a rapid engine of reform. This design for strategic inquiry in large high schools is especially promising when the administration is ready to push change rapidly across key units. Depending on how the school is organized, teams can be constituted in all kinds of ways that bring together teachers who care about and share responsibility for student learning. Most important is to begin where there is energy; these originating teams are pivotal in bringing about change in the school.

The model prompts school administrators and facilitators to think strategically about how to constitute their leading inquiry teams and, especially in large high schools, how to bring along successive teams to broaden and build inquiry leadership.

WHY TARGETS?

Strategic inquiry prompts a team to be explicit about where it wants to go and how exactly it will measure success. Most models for inquiry require a clear, measurable end goal: typically, demonstrated improvement for specific students on a particular summative assessment. Strategic inquiry differs in that it pushes a teacher team to clarify and specify smaller targets along the way through which progress is measured. For example, if the goal is to improve student achievement in algebra, then a team needs to diagnose and focus on particular skill gaps and learning targets, such as division or the concept of substitution, and then evaluate students' response by measuring their improvement on that target. Strategic inquiry prompts a team to break down the teachable/learnable elements of its end goal and to demonstrate progress and make adjustments along the way based on precise information about misconceptions and/or learning needs.

This skill applies to all types of change required by strategic inquiry teams: moving students, moving instructional systems, and moving colleagues. Research on teams' experiences practicing strategic inquiry found that being extremely precise about learning targets is harder for many educators than one might initially expect. Teachers are not used to developing a common understanding of terms, end goals, interim goals, and measures of progress. They are not practiced in breaking down a task into its teachable, measurable components. Nor are they skilled in setting and measuring progress on *learning goals* or *targets*. Our experience confirms that strategic inquiry teams must be led to develop specific learning goals as opposed to generic ones. They need to craft a statement of what exactly students (or colleagues, depending on the nature of the inquiry) will know and be able to do differently, and then to track evidence of learning. We have seen that this is strikingly countercultural for educators, whose default mode, absent guidance and/or practice in creating learning goals, is to create a to-do list—to hold themselves accountable for what they are going to do rather than for results.

The advantage of a team defining learning goals rather than action goals is that doing so helps a strategic inquiry leader or facilitator know what to hold tight and what to hold loose. Strategic inquiry holds tight the learning goal carefully established with evidence, whereas the strategic actions taken to move students, colleagues, or a system toward that goal will shift in response to context and in response to unanticipated reactions to the leaders' actions to make change. Creating and tracking learning targets is crucial to strategic inquiry because it counters the typical demand for compliance with a particular instructional strategy (such as group work) regardless of whether or not there is evidence that it works. If they are skilled and empowered to do so, teachers are best positioned to know how a particular strategy works with students and to adjust it in response to real-time evidence of its impact.

One marker of individuals trained in strategic inquiry is that they are quick to recognize goals that are vague, unmeasurable, or unrealistic. They recognize and reshape closed-loop designs for inquiry that measure effectiveness based on the implementation of a strategy rather than on its impact on student and/or adult learning.

WHAT TASKS?

Successive cycles of inquiry are the heart of strategic inquiry. Inquiry tasks are organized in three distinct but interlocking phases that focus on moving students, moving systems, and moving colleagues. With the exception of the Phase I task of diagnosing a skill gap, the phases are not necessarily rolled out in a linear fashion, even though we number them sequentially.[2] Each shines light on a different aspect of the problem of change and develops the skills and mind-sets needed to address it. Collectively, the three phases comprise the theory of action for strategic inquiry: how teams come to understand how learning conditions work systematically to produce the current sphere of student success, how they act strategically to improve it, and how they spread and embed the capacities needed for continual improvement more broadly and deeply across their school.

Phase I: Move Students

In this phase, a team diagnoses a high-leverage skill gap for specific students outside the sphere of success and then acts and monitors progress from the baseline to the goal for each student and for the group. Team members learn the strategic inquiry cycle, in particular the importance of getting small (specific students, precise skill gap) both to make the work manageable and to ensure learning in an area where they were truly stuck.

Strategic inquiry specifies particular tasks for this phase. First, the team drills down into achievement data to identify a specific group of students outside the school's sphere of success. Ideally, these are students who represent a group for which the school most wishes to improve outcomes. It can be any group of students who are not successful—those who are

FIGURE 1.1   Three interlocking phases of strategic inquiry

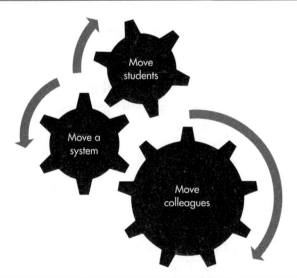

almost successful or far from successful, because, either way, the team/ school will have to learn something new in order to move them toward success. It is best, however, when students are chosen strategically, so that their improvement will give the school a boost in areas in which they are rated, and also when at least some of the students are in the earlier grades of a given school. Focusing instead on students who are about to take a high-stakes summative test (seniors in a high school setting, for example) doesn't afford team members the time they need to engage in deep, new learning. Strategic inquiry balances the need for producing results quickly with the need for time to develop teacher leadership capacity for ongoing change. Inquiry can be applied to students for whom passing a summative exam is pressing and urgent, but the team's learning about more foundational skills, and about high-leverage system responses, will be greater with students who will spend more time in the school.

First, the team uses student record and assessment data to identify a group of students who are struggling academically yet regularly attend the school and to select a small number (twelve to fifteen) of target students for their inquiry work. Drilling down into these students' data—gathered from a range of sources, such as standardized tests, formative assessments, and student work—it identifies a specific skill gap (such as writing). The team then uses evidence to select a more specific subskill (paragraph coherence) and specific learning targets (sequencing, transitions) and articulates a hypothesis: according to current evidence, if students mastered A and B, they will be able to achieve C. Each aspect of the hypothesis must be measurable, so the team develops fine-grained assessments and begins the process of cycles of intervention, assessment, and response to move students toward the larger goal (improved writing).

Focusing the team on a specific learning target is strategic in that it makes the goal of moving students manageable. Before this facet of the design was in place, teams were overwhelmed by the task of analyzing large amounts of data and translating the data into ways of helping students meet grade-level standards. Trained facilitators responded by redesigning the work to focus on a very specific learning target. Absent a push to stay small, some teams gave up on what they perceived as the need to bridge very large skill gaps, doubting that they could make a difference.

This phase of a team's inquiry prompts crucial shifts in teacher beliefs and skills. Many team members start out thinking that the students' gaps are everywhere and that they cannot bridge them. Many believe that the students struggle because of social-emotional problems. Phase I focuses the team's attention on specific skills the students lack that are essential for their success at grade level, skills that can be taught efficiently. They see that the students' learning can be accelerated through inquiry and high-leverage interventions and that their collective ability to articulate learning goals clearly and to create formative assessments to measure progress can help move students who they thought they couldn't move. Teachers also come to see how working on a team supports this process. These perspectives are crucial to their ongoing inquiry and to their change leadership in the school.

Because this work runs counter to teachers' beliefs and school culture in general, it's crucial that a team have a facilitator who is well-grounded in strategic inquiry principles. This person will help the team navigate the predictable challenges it faces during this first phase of the work. A trained facilitator is important in guiding the work in other phases as well, but teams flounder without skilled guidance in Phase I.

Phase II: Move a System

In this phase teams examine and then work to improve at least one instructional decision system in their school. They study, for example, how decisions are made about *what* is taught (curriculum), *who* teaches whom (teacher assignments), or *how* students are assessed and how assessment data are used. By studying decisions through the lens of target students' specific skill gap, identified in Phase I, teams come to see how decisions collectively produce current results ("We don't teach it, so they don't learn it"); how individual actions, including their own, are shaped by larger forces ("I thought it was just me; now I see the pattern and the impact of that pattern on kids"); and how instructional decisions are driven by the school's culture and tradition rather than student needs ("Experienced teachers teach the most successful students; that's how it's always been done around here").

The team identifies a small change that, if successful, would result in target students, and others like them, getting exactly what they had been found to need. This tight focus ensures that decisions will actually improve, since effectiveness is not measured according to the change itself but according to its impact on student learning. And it holds team members accountable for ensuring that their actions have the clearly measurable and intended effect. As in Phase I, team members act in iterative action-reflection cycles to make the work manageable and adjust the next steps in light of evidence. When guided by a trained facilitator, the team learns basic systems principles, such as that a small, strategic change can make a big difference and that everyone has agency for leading change.

An important outgrowth of strategic inquiry over the years is that evidence from almost every team's research has pointed to curriculum as the highest leverage system to be improved. In other words, in almost every case teams have found that, when they get precise enough in their diagnostic work, the specific skill that targeted what students need and lack is not explicitly taught in their school; that the simple act of explicitly teaching those skills is the biggest lever for student improvement; and that mechanisms need to be put in place to continually align curriculum with actual student needs.

In this phase, in order to understand the curriculum as taught in their school (as experienced by target students), a team creates and then analyzes low-inference transcripts (LITs) of target students' classrooms. These verbatim transcripts of everything that is said in a classroom help teachers understand the curriculum as taught and experienced by students, rather than as it exists on a map or in their minds (see appendix B). When the team analyzes LITs through the specific lens of what target students do not know, they are confronted with the reality that these students do not have the opportunity in any of their classes to learn the targeted skills. This process is not about blame but about generating a shared, evidence-based understanding of the current reality of what is systematically taught in relation to what, specifically, students need. LITs are critical in helping teacher teams understand and be able to face this gap squarely and nondefensively. Creating and analyzing LITs generates a shared awareness of this reality and an urgency for change.

Teams also analyze other systems in their school through the lens of struggling students' performance. For example, what happens with assessment information: who typically gets what information, at what level of granularity, and in what form and when? Once a team understands how one or more system works to produce underperformance for specific struggling students, it is ready to identify a particular obstacle to student success and work to change or remove it. The barrier might be, for example, that the student assessment information teachers see is not specific or broken down enough to inform classroom-level responses. One example of a small change that can make a big difference is providing teachers with more specific information about struggling, rather than average, students during meetings.

One powerful system change responded to evidence of the cumulative, negative impact of the common practice in high schools of assigning more experienced teachers to upper-level and more successful students. One team responded by offering its members to teach the most struggling ninth graders the following year, gradually seeding a culture change so that teaching younger and more challenging students came to be seen as desirable. As in Phase I, team members created benchmarks of success and used baseline data to track their progress.

This phase of strategic inquiry develops the team's skills in systems thinking and in mapping the school's systems against students' struggles. It supports shifts in beliefs about why students struggle and what can be done by showing that small changes in the school can make a big difference for student success. It also shifts beliefs about who can lead school change—from the idea that decisions are in the hands of administrators to seeing that all teachers can prompt change for the better. And it shifts thinking about what leading school change is about—from the idea that a grand plan is needed to seeing that strategic choices about change in existing systems and follow-through can have a big impact for students.

Phase III: Move Colleagues

The first two phases of strategic inquiry prepare teachers to lead their colleagues through the process. Phase III frames and supports this challenge of stepping into a leadership role. During this phase teachers branch off from their original inquiry team to lead other colleagues in making the same cultural shifts that they themselves have made toward collective learning, evidence use, shared urgency, and an action orientation for change.

Also during this phase the team members come back together to diagnose and improve their facilitation skills and to get coaching from senior facilitators. As in earlier phases, team members act in cycles of inquiry, defining clear learning goals for their colleagues and evaluating the impact of their own actions and decision making on the desired progress. In Phase III, teachers learn to apply principles for moving students and systems to leading adult learning. They use the same core inquiry process that they used to close skill gaps for students: designing nested, measurable end and interim learning goals and using evidence to track progress and inform next steps in iterative cycles. But they tackle additional challenges as well in taking on a leadership role, often without positional authority, and managing the complexities of the new role, colleague resistance, and so

on. Taking on a change leadership role prompts each team member to become a leader of colleagues, a radical shift from normal collegial relationships. Like in earlier phases, the highly scaffolded nature of the Phase III
task, coupled with support from a trained facilitator, ensures that emerging strategic inquiry leaders are able to navigate these hurdles and take on
the identity of a leader.

WHY FACILITATOR TRAINING?

When undertaking strategic inquiry, schools need a trained facilitator to
guide the initial team's work and develop team members' skills in leading
inquiry with colleagues. Once a team has been through a well-facilitated
process of working through each of the three inquiry phases, its members
should be prepared to facilitate strategic inquiry with other school teams.
In other words, one outcome of going through all three phases of well-
facilitated strategic inquiry—in addition to achievement gains of struggling students, improved school systems, and a spreading of capacity for
evidence-based practice schoolwide—is team members' readiness to lead
inquiry-based school improvement.

Research in New York City schools provides evidence that facilitator
training matters for school progress on inquiry-based reform. The evaluation team's analysis of survey data for schools with and without a facilitator trained in strategic inquiry found that teacher teams' ratings of inquiry
support from a facilitator assigned to their school was a statistically significant predictor of their progress on strategic inquiry.[3] Teachers' reports
in interviews shore up the statistical evidence. Routinely they pointed to
a trained facilitator as crucial in getting their team past the struggles of
learning to implement strategic inquiry. As one teacher put it, "The process
was so frustrating at times that I think if there wasn't an outsider pushing
us, we just would have said: 'No, it's not working.' Or, 'These are just the
types of kids we get. And we're not going to be able to do anything about
it.' Having an outsider to keep pushing us and still *be* there was critical."

Whether an outsider or insider (someone on the school staff), an effective facilitator is deeply grounded in the core principles of strategic in-

quiry and is skilled in adapting the process to the particulars of a given school context in ways that do not compromise the principles or the teams' progress.

What Do They Do?

A facilitator plays somewhat different roles at each phase of strategic inquiry. Although the core inquiry processes are similar across phases, particulars of content and challenges faced are different in each phase, and a team needs specific guidance, tools, and prodding for each. Although no team's progress is exactly the same, there is a typical developmental arc that teams move through as they move across phases. A skilled facilitator adapts her actions in response to a team's learning needs. In general, this requires the facilitator to be highly directive at first and less so over time, shifting to support the team's leadership. As in the gradual release model for classroom instruction, the facilitator begins with "I do" (actively directing them on tasks), then "we do" (working with the team to come up with responses to diagnosed gaps in student skills and instructional systems), and then "you do" (prompting the team to lead colleagues in inquiry and giving advice as requested). Again, this is not completely linear, since each phase entails slightly new challenges and therefore requires some more directive and/or explicit facilitation in the beginning, at least until team members come to see the connection between what they are being asked to do in the current phase and the skills and processes learned in earlier phases.

Phase I is the most challenging for teams and thus for the facilitator, because it is likely to be the teachers' first exposure to strategic inquiry and its counterintuitive ideas and practices. It is most likely in this first phase in which team members do not realize that what they are learning and being asked to do is substantially different from usual practice. Susie Greenebaum, an experienced facilitator, described a typical conversation with a team in Phase I: "It's like you're talking to them from one paradigm, and they're hearing you in another." In this phase it's not unusual, for example, for a facilitator to ask a team, "What is it exactly that your target students cannot do?" and for a team to respond, "We taught them fractions." Or for a facilitator to ask, "How do you know where exactly their learning is falling short?" and for a team to respond, "It's because they do not do their homework."

In Phase I a facilitator must be perfectly clear about the driving purpose and processes required, must recognize different often subtle ways (like the homework response above) that a team can back away from the core task of identifying a clear skill gap with evidence, and must hold to the core process (defining learning goals, taking action, evaluating evidence, etc.) that will push against typical and constraining habits of mind and allow strategic inquiry to do its work of shifting practices and thinking.

In Phase II a team needs explicit teaching about systems thinking and some reminding about the core principles and processes that it is being asked to apply. Now the facilitator can become increasingly less directive, since the team understands from its own experience how getting small can make what otherwise appears overwhelming manageable and can yield new insight. Even with this experience in Phase I, however, a typical team needs help understanding the concept of leverage (how to identify a small place to intervene that will improve a complex system) and trusting it. Though less directive, the facilitator helps a team learn to analyze the school's systems; identify leverage points; create nested, measurable goals for system improvement; and keep at it when change remains hard. This support is crucial to a team's success.

In Phase III (or Phase II, if it comes last), ideally, a facilitator can become even more hands-off, reminding team members that the inquiry process and core strategies are the same but that they need to be applied to adult learning. In the beginning of Phase III, a typical team understands this idea in theory but does not apply it in practice. Even a team that can now use the strategy of getting small effectively to move students and/or a system typically struggles at first to apply the principle to moving adults. The transfer does not happen naturally or on its own without facilitator support. Even a team that has successfully closed skill gaps and improved learning conditions with a specific leverage point, for example, is now likely to identify many general things that teachers on a school inquiry team they are leading need to improve. Or, once the team has identified what needs to improve, it has trouble selecting aligned evidence with which to measure progress. One strategic inquiry leader, for example, wanted her team to have more honest conversations but presented minutes of meetings as her baseline evidence. After having successful experiences in an earlier phase or phases, however, team members experience an *Aha!* when a facilitator points out that they are now getting big, that they need to create learning rather than action goals, and that they need specific evidence relevant to the learning goals—in other words, that the principles they learned earlier do indeed apply to moving colleagues. Many teachers trained in strategic inquiry are shocked to realize how they had, for a time, lost sight of what they'd learned earlier. Having to recall and apply core principles to a new problem is essential for developing deep understanding of strategic inquiry—something the model (and a skilled facilitator) pushes.

How Do They Learn to Do It?

Because most coaches or other individuals in instructional support roles are skilled in content coaching or other approaches to changing teaching practice, they often find it difficult to shift their focus to students and diagnosing skill gaps among struggling students. Like teacher teams beginning strategic inquiry, they typically bring habits of mind and beliefs about how to improve learning that get in the way of effectively facilitating strategic inquiry. Like teachers, individuals in these roles need to experience a full cycle of strategic inquiry in order to learn the deep principles that guide the work. They also need strong facilitation in the process before they can effectively facilitate it. They can get this experience through an aligned certification program, by being part of a team led by a trained facilitator, or by cofacilitating school teams with a trained facilitator. A trained facilitator not only keeps the work on track but models the ways in which a facilitator helps a team navigate the inevitable road blocks and hurdles encountered in learning to do strategic inquiry effectively. In this sense, the model has facilitator training embedded within it, though some strategic inquiry participants will, of course, more naturally gravitate toward and be more skilled in this role.

Beyond initial training, facilitators improve their practice by participating in a team (or learning community) of facilitators. Continuous responsiveness of a facilitator and of the model overall to the complexities of particular contexts requires that facilitators have regular and substantial time to work together to learn, discuss, and revise their work through inquiry.

Key to the success of strategic inquiry in accelerating student achievement is its marriage of school improvement and leadership development. Through its 4 T design—teams, targets, tasks, and training—and the core principle of getting small to get big results, the model improves student achievement by developing a team's leadership to improve decision making across a school. Over time, strategic inquiry develops a culture of shared responsibility, evidence-based practice, and distributed leadership that sustains continuous improvement even in the face of administrative turnover, a changing student population, and shifting policy contexts.

CHAPTER 2

How Strategic Inquiry Pays Off

New York City has been a testing ground for strategic inquiry for nearly a decade. Schools began sending teacher teams to the Baruch College certification program in 2005–2006, and then, in 2007–2008, the city's department of education rolled out the model for inquiry-based improvement districtwide. What ensued was wide variation in how well NYC schools implemented strategic inquiry due to differences in principal buy-in and knowledge of the model and how to support it, uneven training and skills among those in facilitator roles, and whether or not the school invested in developing teachers' inquiry leadership.

This variation in New York City schools' implementation offers an opportunity for investigating how and under what circumstances strategic inquiry improves student performance and develops a school's capacity to sustain progress. To assess student effects, the evaluation team compared success rates for high- versus low-implementation schools. And to evaluate school culture effects, the team tracked change on capacity indicators for the high-implementation schools over time.[1] We summarize results relevant to three key empirical questions:

- Do schools that implement strategic inquiry as intended do better on measures of student success, as compared to weak implementers?

- Do teachers in high-implementation schools shift their beliefs about struggling students and their ability to make a difference, as intended?

- Do high-implementation schools shift their culture toward shared accountability, evidence-based practice, and distributed leadership, as intended?

GETTING STUDENTS ON TRACK

The design for strategic inquiry requires that a school team first move specific struggling students and then remove constraints in the system, with the intended effect of "bringing more students into success." Therefore, to determine whether schools did better as a result of strategic inquiry, the evaluation team needed a measure of getting students up to grade-level performance standards for high schools, of getting students on track for graduation and college readiness. In New York City, as elsewhere, being "on track" means meeting basic or proficient standards for grade-level performance in core academic subjects on the annual state test, getting passing grades in courses required for graduation, and passing some sort of exit exam (in New York, getting a minimum score on each of the required state Regents exams).

To see if strategic inquiry improves student outcomes, evaluators wanted to know if there is evidence that strategic inquiry helps a school get struggling students (those off track when they entered the school) on track for graduation by the time they enter twelfth grade. For statistical evaluation, the team used an on-/off-track status measure ("off track," "almost on track," "on track for graduation," and "on track for college") for those students who had come into the school with reading and math scores below grade level in the eighth grade.[2] Data were the 2011 on-/off-track statuses for students in the 2012 graduating class (who were juniors in 2011, unless held back).

The evaluation team needed a comparison group in order to address the question of whether schools implementing strategic inquiry did better than they would have without investing in the model for several years. To establish a comparison group, the team used rigorous methods to identify high schools that differed in their implementation of strategic inquiry but were otherwise similar in order to keep everything that might affect schools' success with students at risk of failure the same *other than* their investment in strategic inquiry for at least three years. (The developmental theory of change suggests that significant results for students would show up around the third year of implementation.) First, the team identified schools that met implementation criteria of having involved successive teacher teams in training with a skilled facilitator (one trained in the credentialing program) and authorized them to lead colleagues in strategic inquiry. This yielded a sample of 13 high-implementation schools in a subdistrict serving 80 schools, which then were "matched" with 13 low-implementation schools in the same subdistrict, schools where teachers were assigned to inquiry teams but, as of 2011, lacked a trained facilitator to guide teams and help develop inquiry leadership. Pairs of high- versus low-implementation schools were matched on size (large or small) and on a school composition index that combined the percentages of students who are poor (eligible for free and reduced-price meals), from a specific race/ethnic group (white, black, Hispanic, and Asian), and at-risk of not graduating (having scored "Below Basic" in reading and in mathematics in eighth grade, prior to entering the high school).

Results of the comparison of on-/off-track statuses for students below grade level when they entered the school support the prediction that strategic inquiry accelerates the academic growth of struggling students. The pie charts in figure 2.1 show that high schools implementing strategic inquiry for three or more years far outperformed matched comparison schools that were relatively weak in implementation.

In the strategic inquiry high schools, a much larger proportion of students who entered with eighth grade test scores below grade level were, by eleventh grade, on track to graduate from high school and go on to college and careers. In these schools, 24 percent of students who entered "at risk" were on track for college readiness, versus 10 percent in the comparison schools. A substantial difference also shows up in the proportion of students seriously off track for graduation—25 percent in the strategic inquiry schools versus 38 percent in comparison schools. At both ends of the student performance spectrum, schools that invested in strategic inquiry did better than their counterparts. In fact, our analyses found that students entering schools which had been practicing strategic inquiry

FIGURE 2.1   Strategic inquiry brings struggling students on track for graduation and college readiness.

Students' on-track statuses

Strategic inquiry schools

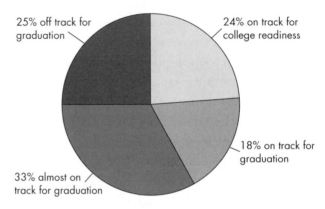

25% off track for graduation

24% on track for college readiness

18% on track for graduation

33% almost on track for graduation

Matched comparison schools

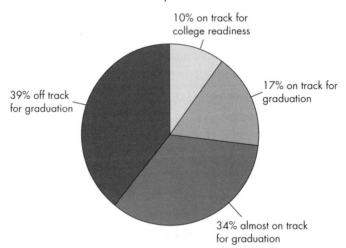

10% on track for college readiness

39% off track for graduation

17% on track for graduation

34% almost on track for graduation

Note: On-track statuses in 2011 are compared for students in the 2012 graduation cohort who scored below grade level in reading and in math in the eighth grade (struggling students when they entered high school). The strategic inquiry and comparison school groups each include thirteen schools. Comparison schools were matched with strategic inquiry schools on size and a School Comparison Index.

for three or more years had an increased likelihood of being on track to graduation, approximately as much as if they had entered with relatively high reading scores.[3] The extraordinary performance of two large restructured high schools that heavily invested in the model (trend data for these schools included in figure 2.1) suggests that strategic inquiry may be especially promising as a reform strategy for such schools.

SHIFTING TEACHERS' MIND-SETS

Change literature often suggests that belief systems dictate improvement and, therefore, that teachers must come to hold certain beliefs (that all students can learn, for example) as a condition for improvement. Strategic inquiry assumes that teachers' beliefs and practices change through experiences that disconfirm earlier beliefs. It is designed to bring them through a highly structured set of tasks that engage them in the actual work of school improvement and through which they can experience success. Team members who diagnose and close skill gaps for students who have been persistently unsuccessful come to change their opinion about the reasons these and other students have failed and about their own ability to serve them. When they make a small but strategic systemic change that benefits a larger group of similar students, they come to believe in their own agency and the ability of any person to make a difference, even those without positional authority. Actual improvement brings about a shift in beliefs (rather than vice versa); new beliefs then accelerate improvement by motivating teams to refine their inquiry skills and involve their colleagues.

Evidence regarding shifts in teacher beliefs and school culture comes from the evaluation team's longitudinal research as well as action research by successive teams of facilitators in the Baruch College credentialing program. Quantitative data are from six years of annual teacher surveys measuring trends on school culture dimensions (administered in approximately eighty schools that are part of the New Visions subdistrict) as well as from the city's department of education ratings on the Quality Review, which includes measures of inquiry team practice. Qualitative evidence comes from case studies of twelve of these high schools, documenting each school's experiences implementing strategic inquiry over three to five years through interviews and observations of inquiry team meetings. At the same time, facilitators in the SAM credentialing program, which spawned strategic inquiry, carried out action research over five program iterations. In weekly meetings they used their own strategic inquiry process to continuously improve their work to meet the learning needs of their teams and schools. They analyzed data from school teams' work to identify patterns of struggle and then respond—by adjusting the design for either inquiry teams' work or facilitation practice. Specific shifts in teachers' beliefs and in school culture repeatedly showed up in the six high-implementation evaluation sites and were corroborated by the teams' reports to their facilitators. When asked about changes they have experienced through strategic inquiry, teachers routinely make comments such as:

> I used to think that the starting point for dealing with struggling students should be asking why, in socioemotional terms, they are struggling. Now I think that looking at student work and making instructional decisions based on the work should be our starting point in trying to reach struggling students. (High school English teacher)

> I used to think that a certain proportion of my math students wouldn't be able to pass the exam no matter what. Now I think that by modifying my instruction I can reach many of the struggling students . . . I discovered that my students were capable of so much more than I thought possible. (High school math teacher)

Such growth in teacher efficacy comes about through their experience working as part of a school inquiry team led and leveraged by a trained strategic inquiry facilitator. Our research shows that key shifts happen in teacher teams across diverse schools, usually within the first year.

From Teaching to Student Learning

A key shift that occurs fairly rapidly in the strategic inquiry process is that teachers change their focus from teaching (implementing a curriculum, using particular grouping strategies, creating new ways of questioning students) to learning—how students are doing and what skills they need to access the curriculum and meet standards. When they begin the inquiry process, teachers often have trouble seeing the distinction, since, of course, the two are intertwined. After a short time they come to realize that they have focused primarily on *what* and *how* they are teaching—on whether they'd delivered the content, for example, or on whether or not they'd done so using a particular best practice—but not on whether or not their students had learned. This is a big shift in teachers' thinking, especially at the secondary level, where teachers generally think of themselves as content-area specialists and where they are pressed to follow a pacing guide that culminates in a high-stakes exam.

Most teachers who become involved in strategic inquiry report that their thinking about instruction changes. In interviews, teachers consistently report—and observations corroborate—that they pay less attention than before to what they are supposed to teach or how they are supposed to teach it and more attention to evidence of what exactly students need and whether or not their current practices work. When they observed instruction, they paid less attention to what the teacher was delivering and more attention to how instruction was landing on students. They paid less attention to the group overall and more attention to specific students, especially those struggling the most.

Teachers on inquiry teams learn that their prior ideas about "high-quality" teaching don't necessarily mesh with struggling students' learning needs; that struggling students miss essential foundational skills; and that the current curriculum often does not provide an opportunity for students to learn those skills. They find that when students are taught those missing skills, their learning accelerates. Teachers learn that they can make no assumptions about what each student knows and needs and that they must make continual adjustments in curriculum maps, including incorporating needed skills and trimming down numbers of topics to go into more depth in order to raise more students up to standard.

From Summative to Formative Assessments of Student Learning

Strategic inquiry prompts teachers to develop an appetite for and skill in creating and using fine-grained assessments to identify struggling students' skill gaps and to measure progress resulting from their interventions. Teachers say that "before" they had seen data as cold, as a tool useful in sorting or sanctioning students, but they came to understand that different types of assessments are useful for different kinds of educational decisions and that the grain size of current assessments is generally insufficient for informing classroom-level next steps. Summative assessments do not provide quality information about what a student needs to learn next and/or the misconceptions currently impeding understanding of a specific learning goal.

Early on teacher teams involved in strategic inquiry learn to adapt existing data on student and school performance to create new ways of getting needed information and to view everything they do (lessons, activities, conversations with students) as *formative assessment* to use in determining their next steps. The intended shift is from designing tests primarily for grading purposes to using formative assessments to diagnose student learning needs and develop and evaluate instructional responses.

Teachers tell us—and our survey data confirm—that they have gotten better at detecting students' misconceptions and knowledge gaps and at creating responses to accelerate their learning. They also have gotten better at scaffolding learning objectives for their lessons and prompting students to give them feedback on struggles with particular content. In addition, they have learned to use inquiry as a problem-solving tool for other school-related problems and have come to understand the critical role of assessments in better understanding the problem at hand and tracking process.

From External Attributions of Student Failure to Instructional Efficacy

A crucial intended outcome is that teachers stop perceiving student failure as something beyond their control. Many teachers in poor urban schools believe that their struggling students fall and stay behind because of miserable family circumstances or personal troubles. Further, especially in high schools where struggling students often test way below their grade level on academic measures, teachers often feel overwhelmed and at a loss over how to effectively respond, concluding that students can never catch up and/or that there is nothing teachers can do to help.

This manifests in teachers' typical resistance to the press in early phases of strategic inquiry to diagnose a precise learning gap. Early on they say things like, "But I know what the problem is, that Student X isn't motivated." Later, once a precise skill gap is pinpointed and teachers are then pressed to determine whether or not that needed skill is taught, resistance typically resurfaces. When a facilitator holds the team tight to the process, however, allowing them to see clear cause-effect relationships—that in fact the needed skill is not taught and that when it is taught directly students learn it—participants experience a revelation. These *"Aha! moments"* occur suddenly and dramatically and are reinforced when participants see teachers in other inquiry teams having a similar experience.

Once a teacher team has learned to diagnose and respond to students' specific skill gaps and sees the academic gains the students then make, teachers develop a sense of instructional efficacy that carries over into their classrooms. This is something we have seen happen over and over. The process shifts their views about the issue of student motivation; they come to see it not as the problem itself but, rather, as a symptom of disconnect between what's provided and what struggling students need.

From Jargon to Precise Language

Another intended outcome of strategic inquiry is that teachers come to demand sense-making among themselves. Often in the current environment, teachers are scrambling to make sense of competing mandates and/or theories of change—for example, to refocus attention to the most struggling students to close achievement gaps and, at the same time, to develop more rigorous curriculum and raise the bar for even the best-performing students to meet the new Common Core State Standards.

Although these team purposes are not contradictory in theory—almost everyone agrees on the ultimate goal of getting all students to meet rigorous standards—the question is more about how teachers are to make sense of conflicting theories of *how* they and the system as a whole will move from where we are to where we need to be and to identify the priorities for teacher learning. Just when teachers are beginning to shift focus to learning gaps for struggling students, they are being pulled to develop more rigorous curriculum and instruction that, unless they've learned to diagnose and close the gaps, will leave these very students farther behind. We've observed this pattern in some NYC schools and in other districts new to inquiry-based improvement approaches.

As a result of this confusion, teachers often use language reflecting the various mandates that they do not fully understand. What exactly is meant by "inquiry" as promoted by the district? What does "rigor" of student learning mean and look like in practice? A word like *rigor* may seem clear at first, but, when pressed, teachers come to see that it is not so clear. For example, does teaching foundational skills that students lack qualify as "rigorous instruction"? Teachers need to come to an understanding and agreement in order to know where they want students to go, teach effectively to that end, and monitor and measure progress.

Teacher teams engaged in strategic inquiry learn to be clear about where exactly they are going and how they will know where they are. They learn to challenge each other's language, check assumptions, and press for precision to ensure that what was known, and not yet known, is clear to everyone.

Figure 2.2 captures the particular shifts in beliefs and practices experienced by the teachers we studied when they worked on strategic inquiry with a school team. The shifts are leveraged and supported by both the design for inquiry and skilled facilitation of inquiry cycles.

CHANGING SCHOOL CULTURE

The shifts in teachers' beliefs and efficacy that strategic inquiry brings about both respond to and advance their team's skills in using the process to improve student achievement. A team's success helps spread strategic inquiry practice across the school. Even in schools we observed that had only one teacher team using strategic inquiry, their successful interventions for struggling students spread when colleagues heard of the learning gains. Colleagues' appetite for becoming part of an inquiry team also grew.

FIGURE 2.2 How strategic inquiry changes teacher beliefs and practice

Outcomes	From . . .	To . . .
Focus on student learning	Focus on curriculum delivery and teaching practice	Focus on student learning and access to instructional content
Formative assessment of student learning	Use of summative assessments to evaluate and grade student performance	Use of formative assessments to diagnose student learning needs and evaluate instruction
Sense of efficacy	Belief that students struggle because of external factors; a sense of helplessness to make a difference	Belief that struggling students have skill gaps that can be addressed; a sense of confidence in helping all students succeed
Use of clear, precise language	Acceptance of jargon and/ or top-down mandates without checking for common understanding	Development of clear, common definitions of terms and goals; use of simple, precise language

Schools that pursued strategic inquiry for several years and involved multiple teacher teams in using the collaborative inquiry model reached a "tipping point" in their school culture after about the third year. This comes about as a critical mass of teachers becomes skilled in using strategic inquiry to improve student success and as they take on roles of leading change in their school. These schools are now places where teachers share accountability for improving student achievement, use evidence of student learning needs to make decisions about instruction, and take on roles and identities as leaders.

Toward Shared Accountability

I used to think that one teacher alone could make dramatic differences in the lives of their students, and now I think that students' lives and futures are better changed when all of their teachers are communicating and supporting the skills taught in one another's classrooms.

High school science teacher

Teachers sharing accountability for student success flies in the face of the profession's long-standing privacy norms. It calls on teachers to shift from thinking of themselves as responsible and accountable for just what goes on in their classroom and requires them to open up to learning with and from their colleagues, to get past feeling inadequate and vulnerable to criticism or feeling superior and unwilling to share knowledge and resources.

Strategic inquiry leverages a shift in school culture to shared accountability within each teacher team. Working together to improve the success of a specific group of struggling students prompts team members to become mutually accountable. Engaging in a process of real learning as a team, they become practiced being public with what they do not know and taking action even with incomplete information. Ultimately, teachers hold themselves and their teammates accountable for generating, testing, and refining ideas that result in moving a specific group of struggling students to higher achievement.

By involving successive teams in these practices, inquiry leaders brought about a shift in the school culture. In these schools, the faculty came to see collaboration and shared responsibility to improve student achievement as "the way we do things here."

Toward Evidence-Based Practice

I used to think that in order to be a better teacher I had to learn and keep up with all the newest bells and whistles, and now I think that all the bells and whistles only work if you have clear learning objectives and evidence of learning.

High school math teacher

Despite the buzz about data use and evidence-based practice in education, shifting school culture in this direction poses daunting challenges. First, many teachers are not comfortable with or experienced in using data. Apart from the technical challenges of interpreting data, some teachers distrust data because they equate the term with standardized tests that don't measure student learning objectives well or effectively inform their instruction. Others see the purpose of student performance data in terms of rating and grading students' mastery of subject matter taught (expecting a bell curve distribution), instead of providing a way to diagnose students' learning needs. (Oddly, the public may generally hold the view that educational tests are useful mainly for ranking students and rating teachers and schools, in contrast with the view that medical tests are useful mainly for diagnosing and improving client health outcomes.) Even with the current emphasis on creating new formative assessment tracking systems, such as the quarterly benchmark assessments that most districts now administer, the data they yield are often not sufficiently granular to inform next steps, and teachers are often swamped in piles of data but not trained or skilled in how to use them well.

Strategic inquiry works because it holds school teams to its core principle of getting small in order to diagnose specific student learning needs. Staying small helps teacher teams cut through the reams of available data to zoom in on strategic targets. As one teacher put it:

> The thing we do [now] without thinking twice is, when you assess the kids it's: "What do they know? What do they not know? What do they almost know?" And that's where you start, with a skill—"What do they almost know." They have the idea of it, but they haven't mastered it yet. After they master that, then the "thing they didn't know" becomes the next thing that they can master.

Teacher teams that develop this kind of diagnosis and intervention practice learn to make use of what's available to make strategic choices: to recognize the limits of available data and then tweak it or create new assessments to get needed information. In other words, they become skilled detectives in search of answers to important problems; they use specific data to answer their questions, rather than drowning in massive data. Leadership to spread this experience is pivotal to bringing about change in the broader school culture.

Toward Distributed Leadership

I used to think that administrators were able to set and adjust the culture of a school through leadership, and now I think that a school's culture is only as positive [for student learning] as all members of its community make it.

High school English teacher

Broad, or "distributed," leadership is by now a tenet for school improvement. There is wide agreement, grounded in research and practice, that the immense challenges involved in bringing school-level capacity from where it is to where it needs to be to bring all students to standard requires strong leadership at all levels of school functioning. Strategic inquiry takes this idea one step further, however, through its design for teacher teams to take leadership in working to transform their schools from the ground up, even where district and/or school administrative leadership is weak. Strong leadership at every level of the system is ideal. Schools will not become the engines of improvement that they need to be unless notions of leadership as vested only in positional authority—the idea that you can only forge improvement if you have a leadership title and/or the idea that a superstar leader can do it alone—change.

Strategic inquiry develops individual and team leadership for school improvement. Its stance is that everyone has agency and thus the ability and responsibility to make change. Its principle of staying small makes change efforts manageable, traceable, and strategic. When teachers take leadership roles in their inquiry teams, their ideas about school leadership shift; they move from seeing administrators as having sole authority and prerogative for making decisions to feeling that teachers have agency and responsibility for improving student achievement.

Schools that persisted with strategic inquiry for several years showed a trajectory of growth in teacher leadership of collaborative inquiry over time—a condition key to sustaining the practice and culture. In turn, inquiry leadership engendered teachers' use of assessment data to guide instruction across the school. Annual teacher surveys captured this trend for four schools that involved successive teacher teams in strategic inquiry and developed broad inquiry leadership. Figure 2.3 shows each school's scores on a survey measure of assessment use to measure student progress and to evaluate their curriculum and instruction. The data show that the schools reached a tipping point toward an inquiry culture in the third year, after which the upward trend on the assessment use plateaued. However, this survey measure does not capture the deepening use of data that we observed in these schools.

FIGURE 2.3   Impact of strategic inquiry on school culture of assessment use, 2006–2011

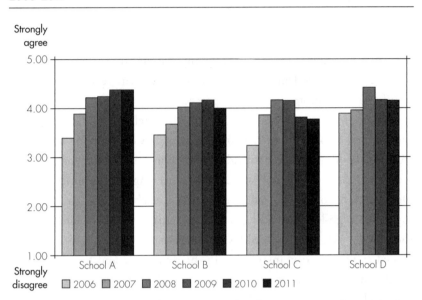

Note: A school's score for each year is the average of teacher responses on a five-point scale to two survey statements: "We use a variety of assessment strategies to measure student progress" and "We use assessment data to evaluate our curriculum and instructional practices."

Toward a Learning Stance and Appetite for Professional Development

A few years ago, I went to a PD [professional development] on teaching writing across the content areas, and I remember thinking, "This just doesn't relate to me and my students." I barely paid attention. Now I see how the literacy strategies we're learning [in the PD] meet the exact skill gaps we uncovered in inquiry, and I'm getting better and better at using them.

High school social studies teacher

One by-product of teachers' greater agency and efficacy in meeting student needs is that they become smarter about curriculum and better consumers of professional development. If they identify a significant student skill gap that is not addressed in their curriculum and teaching, teacher teams seek the help of outside experts. Their appetite for learning comes from the need to teach important skills to struggling students. This is a sea change from typical professional development regimens that deliver training to teachers because someone in the district or school administration decides they need particular new knowledge or skills. By implication, strategic inquiry builds a bridge between students' learning needs and teachers' learning needs and specific kinds of professional development.

In some mature strategic inquiry schools, teacher teams converged in their efforts to address particular skill gaps prevalent among struggling students, prompting a schoolwide instructional response. For example, after three years of inquiry within small learning communities in New Dorp High School, team leaders across SLCs reached consensus that writing was a high-leverage skill domain not currently taught effectively in the school. Teachers in all SLCs, spanning subject areas, were eager to embed explicit writing instruction in their curricula and for professional development to support their learning to effectively teach it. Principal DeAngelis brokered a series of on-site professional development days with a literacy/writing expert whose work was enthusiastically received. This learning agenda grew out of teachers' diagnosis of their student learning needs, rather than from school administrators' judgments. DeAngelis commented on the shift:

> I used to empty out the school. "Yeah, go to that workshop. Go to that workshop. Come back, turn-key it." The bottom line is, it never really gets turn-keyed. People pick up on one or two tricks from wherever they went, and they put it in their bag of tricks, and they use it from time to time. But they never walk away with a more enriched classroom. They never walk away and develop a more enriched classroom from a workshop or series of workshops . . . So the bandaid approach really doesn't work.

Developing a school culture of shared accountability, evidence-based practice, and distributed leadership means shifting professional norms away from what has been typical in U.S. schools toward new expectations and routines. Figure 2.4 highlights the key normative shifts that strategic inquiry engenders.

FIGURE 2.4   How strategic inquiry changes school culture

Outcomes	From . . .	To . . .
Shared accountability	"My students"	"Our students"
	Typical, successful student	Specific struggling students
Evidence-based practice	Decisions based on intuition and past practice	Decisions made and evaluated using data on student outcomes
Distributed leadership	Leadership vested in formal position	Everyone has agency and responsibility for student success
	Top-down decisions	Teacher leadership and team decision making

These shifts in "the way we do things in our school" interact over time with the shifts in teachers' beliefs and perspectives (see figure 2.2). For example, as school teams come to share accountability for improving struggling students' success, individuals shift from a view of teaching as delivering a curriculum to teaching as diagnosing and addressing students' learning needs. Conversely, as teachers experience success in moving struggling students, the norms of evidence-based practice and shared accountability take root in the school. The individual and cultural shifts here are iterative and gradual. They come about as school teams learn to use inquiry to diagnose and improve student achievement. Each shift is worked at and supported by each phase of strategic inquiry. Each is crucial for sustaining inquiry-based school improvement.

We have found that school teams' progress on strategic inquiry is not linear; rather, it is bumpy and cyclical. As teachers move outside their comfort zone to develop new assessment and instructional practices, they grapple with the tug of old habits and mind-sets. Teachers report moving "two steps forward and one step back," needing to "relearn" a new practice and perspective. They experience an *Aha!* only to then encounter a new challenge. Some teams get stymied by the roadblocks they encounter and never get beyond superficial routines of data use; others become highly skilled in using data to continuously improve student learning and success.

DOING WHAT IT TAKES TO BRING ABOUT INQUIRY-BASED SCHOOL REFORM

Schools that embrace strategic inquiry should be clear about what they are getting into and what it takes for administrators and other school leaders to develop the faculties' capacity for ongoing inquiry-based improvement. Fundamental are sustained investment in developing teacher teams' inquiry skills, creating time for inquiry and the opportunity for teacher leadership to grow, and fighting against strong currents in American education that work against collaborative, evidence-based practice in schools. Partnering with an external and/or internal facilitator trained in strategic inquiry is key to navigating the challenges of capacity building and culture change.

Developing Teachers' Inquiry Skills

Teacher teams struggle in developmentally predictable ways—given current culture and context—at each phase of strategic inquiry. In the beginning, they struggle with sorting through massive amounts of data to identify a high-leverage area of focus. Required to be more specific in diagnosing skill gaps, teams struggle with the challenge of making sense of current information (understanding what wrong answers on a test can tell them, for example) and with adapting tests or generating new assessments to provide useful information to inform their next steps. This is a huge gap in the knowledge of teachers and in the education field as a whole—and given that assessments generally are not sufficiently granular to serve the needs of classroom teachers, strategic inquiry develops these skills in large measure to fill the gaps in larger assessment systems.

A team's ability to get up and running on inquiry cycles depends in part on having an assessment-savvy person to lead the work. This could be a school administrator or a teacher specialist who has been trained to use a district data system to disaggregate results (such as NYC schools' designated data specialists). A common challenge, however, is that a data-savvy person may be knowledgeable about data systems and large-scale data but not skilled in sorting the information so that important patterns will emerge, and they may not be trained in knowing the limits of existing data to provide answers for the questions the data generate. External facilitators or school leaders and/or data specialists with these sorts of assessment skills are needed to get teacher teams past the frustrations of learning to use data diagnostically.

One data specialist described his evolving understanding of his role in strategic inquiry: "I used to start the year giving all my teachers a big binder of data and I thought I'd done my job. They wanted data; they got data! Now I know they need help making meaning from the information—and that I have to be more selective and really understand what they need and why."

As they move through the phases of strategic inquiry, teacher teams need help developing a systems perspective—specifically, in identifying a small, high-leverage intervention, acting on the idea that a small change can make a big difference.

In both areas of challenge—developing assessment skills and developing systems knowledge and skills—teacher teams depend on a facilitator who is well trained in strategic inquiry to keep them from getting stuck and discouraged. Recall the teacher who told us that her team's early struggles were so frustrating that they would have given up without their facilitator's support.

Creating Time and Teacher Leadership

Teacher teams need regular dedicated time for their inquiry work. Yet site administrators manage competing priorities for teachers' time and work outside the classroom. Among schools involved in strategic inquiry, we found wide variation in both frequency and reliability of time designated for teacher inquiry. Some teams floundered because their scheduled meeting time was often co-opted for another purpose, such as planning for summer school or professional development for a curriculum project. Absent a school priority for collaborative inquiry and protection of the schedule, the work stalls. If the initiative is seen just as a district priority, then teachers take a compliance mentality.

The principal's commitment to and priority for strategic inquiry is pivotal to its success in changing the school culture. Even if she or he is unprepared to lead the work, the principal must understand the principles and believe that it is an effective vehicle for instructional improvement. In schools where the principal was on board and strategic in involving external facilitators and developing teacher-leaders, teams became effective—once-struggling students became more successful, and the school culture tipped in about three years. In others it didn't take root. This does not imply that the primary change agent in successful schools was the principal; indeed, broad or distributed leadership is fundamental to inquiry-based reform. But a principal's willingness to share decision authority is essential if collaborative inquiry is to take root.

Fighting Against Strong Currents in American Education

Teachers' professional norms, views of teaching quality reflected in current education policy, and prevailing notions of student success work against the agenda put forth by strategic inquiry. They push against teacher collaboration to ensure all students' success. Strategic inquiry is designed to take on these inhibitors of change by organizing the work in ways that shift educators' mind-sets and professional relations away from the status quo. School administrators play a key role in leading and supporting change. Among the countervailing forces are:

- *The norm of individualized teacher practice.* Perhaps the most powerful inhibitor of collaboration in most schools today is that teaching has long been viewed and carried out as an individual practice. Research has repeatedly documented the strong privacy norm in our nation's teaching culture (in contrast to norms in countries with more positive outcomes, such as Singapore and Finland). This means that individual teachers are expected to develop their instructional practices and judge their students' progress on their own. Shoring up this norm is the recent policy push to isolate individual teachers' contributions to student growth. This evaluation strategy assumes that teacher competition, rather than collaboration, will advance educational achievement and equity.

• *Prescribed curriculum and instruction.* In recent years, the ideal of evidence-based teaching practice has gravitated toward the idea of "what works" and a one-size-fits-all approach to educational improvement. Under NCLB, states were pressed to screen education programs on the basis of documented overall effects on student learning and then require districts to adopt one of the selected "evidence-based" curricula. In turn, districts required teachers to implement the adopted curricula "with fidelity." This improvement strategy assumes that teachers' diagnoses and judgments about what and how their students need to learn don't matter much for their students' success.

• *The sorting function of education.* Educators live in a society that prizes competition among individuals and assumes that some will be successful and some will fail. They inherit a K–12 educational culture that was designed to screen individuals for a highly stratified higher education system and that allows many to fall by the wayside. In this culture, education assessments are a sorting mechanism to ensure the best learning opportunities for the highest-performing students. Although NCLB holds schools and districts accountable to show gains for all student subgroups, and thus surfaces patterns of inequality, this legislation doesn't come close to shifting the received mission of schools and mind-sets of educators and their constituencies.

School and civic leaders who invest in strategic inquiry and evidence-based decision making as the promise for public education reform must fight against these currents in American education. Facilitators who work with teacher teams to develop their skills and sense of efficacy to move struggling students also must push against them.

Indeed, our research found that school teams that successfully made the journey to an inquiry culture were supported by an external facilitator or teacher-leader who deeply understood its core principles, the kinds of trouble a team is likely to encounter, and facilitation strategies to move the team forward. As a design for developing evidence-based practice in a school, strategic inquiry therefore calls for a considerable investment in time for facilitator training and support, since they also need to engage in ongoing processes to develop new skills and new beliefs.

Strategic inquiry takes on the challenge of overcoming powerful institutional constraints on inquiry-based school improvement. Its design for school teams' inquiry is strategic in shifting educators' thinking about relationships with colleagues, quality instruction, and struggling students. It guides school teams over the hurdles to developing their capacity to bring about steady improvement in student achievement.

PART II

STRATEGIC INQUIRY IN ACTION

Strategic inquiry develops team leadership for school improvement through its three distinct and interlocking phases. This section's chapters illustrate how a school team moves through each phase (moving students, moving systems, moving colleagues) by highlighting the developmentally predictable challenges teams typically confront and illustrating how the core principles and design elements of strategic inquiry, including strategic facilitation, work to support teams' progress through them.

Each chapter focuses on one phase and highlights the challenges that, if not effectively navigated, most threaten to derail the work. The facilitator role is most crucial during a team's initial exposure to the model and so is featured prominently in the first chapter. The descriptions of facilitator thinking and strategy are intended to shed light on where teams typically get stuck and to highlight core design elements that are most frequently avoided or misunderstood absent strategic facilitator intervention.

CHAPTER 3

Moving Students to Succeed

Most teams begin the strategic inquiry process in Phase I, which prompts them to work collaboratively to identify and close learning gaps for struggling students. Typically a team is challenged by almost every facet of this task: drilling down into available data to identify focal students, creating granular assessments, and acting in evidence-based cycles to move students forward. The most challenging aspects, however, are those that are most particular to the tight focus necessary to inform improvement specifically, the requirement that diagnostics are precise enough to yield new information about what *exactly* struggling students need next.

Team members are challenged by the model's demands for collaborative learning as well. They are asked to focus on what they do not know: areas of school struggle rather than success; student learning rather than teacher practice; and assumptions that limit rather than promote student success. Further, they face external pressures for immediate results that can threaten school progress on strategic inquiry by creating an urgency versus capacity building dilemma.

In Phase I, strategic facilitation is essential for helping teams new to the work to navigate these challenges. The design elements alone are insufficient for making the needed difference. Most challenging for the typical team is making the shift to a focus on student learning and using the model's core strategy of getting small to do so. Facilitators play a crucial role in holding teams to those aspects of the design that are most coun-terintuitive and that they are most likely to evade but that are also key in prompting the desired shifts. In doing so, facilitators model a focus on what matters most and the kinds of context-dependent strategic decision making that team members come to internalize and to apply indepen-dently in later phases.

In Phase I, teams struggle in particular with their selection of target stu-dents and with how precise their diagnostic of these students' learning gaps must get. Here we illustrate how each of these challenges typically manifest and the kinds of facilitator thinking and moves.

HOW TO FOCUS ON STUDENT LEARNING: WHICH STUDENTS SHOULD WE FOCUS ON?

Decisions about which students to focus on are important to teacher learn-ing, focal students' learning, and, ultimately, the effectiveness of larger, systemic changes informed by Phase I. These decisions have a lot riding on them. They are thorny because the team needs to confront and navigate the urgency/capacity building dilemma, to make decisions about whether to prioritize teacher capacity building or moving students in a particu-lar moment in time. Where a team comes down in this decision reflects both the realities of the specific context and moment and the priorities and theories of change in play. Strategic inquiry addresses both immedi-ate and long-term needs while adapting to context demands, but leans to-ward capacity building in many instances in which other reform models might prioritize what seems urgent. The examples illustrate how this ten-sion emerges in particular contexts as well as the challenge and possibility of prioritizing teacher learning. They show how strategic facilitation helps a team shift to prioritizing learning and reap the benefits of improved stu-dent performance as well.

Selecting Target Students at the Start of the Process

The urgency/capacity building dilemma surfaced almost immediately at Jefferson, a large New York City high school.[1] The school had called in

Deanna, a strategic inquiry facilitator, to strengthen an inquiry process that had been in place for two years but that leaders worried wasn't getting "deep enough." Although Jefferson had previously restructured into eight smaller learning communities, each with a daily common planning period with time for inquiry team work, it had just been labeled a Restart High School, which gave their inquiry added urgency to be effective. The federal designation came with a threat of sanctions—if the school didn't improve on key accountability measures quickly it would be closed—but it also came with funds for support. They brought in Deanna as a key element of this support.

Early on Deanna facilitated SLC leaders in a simulated activity to select focal students and then in a discussion of how to shape the selection of focal students for each of their teams. They were asked to bring a list of ten to twenty target students for each team (each SLC had two to five teacher teams) along with each team's evidence-based rationale. Given the particulars of each SLC, including how leaders had constituted teacher teams (grade level versus subject area, strengths, personalities, etc), each leadership pair would determine how and how strictly to structure this process.

As a model, Deanna provided the following guidelines for a team's selection of "focal students." Focal students must:

- Be outside the sphere of success, not currently successful in meeting grade-level standards

- Have good attendance, so we can learn from them about instruction

- Be struggling in a common essential skill gap

- Be in the ninth or tenth grade (for maximum impact)

- Be selected through a process that maximizes teacher buy-in (so that all team members have a vested interest in them and/or the target skill), and benefits the school's accountability measures (be strategic in terms of meeting AYP standards).

As SLC leaders grappled with the question of how best to shape this complex process, they immediately confronted the urgency/capacity building dilemma: Nate spoke to the group, in Deanna's presence and said, "We know who we have to move. We've identified two hundred seniors who are in danger of not graduating. We have to focus on them. If we don't improve our graduation rate this year, we could be closed."

Deanna reiterated the guidelines and the brief explanation of the reasons, but Nate was firm. He said, "These are the students we have to move. The stakes are very high. This is what we're being held accountable for not sometime in the future but right now. And we know who they are. I can give you their names."

The group was quiet. They seemed willing to defer to Nate's expertise (he had been the leader of inquiry prior to Deanna's coming on board) and to the reality he spoke about. Graduation rates were being closely watched. It was hard to argue that focusing on seniors wasn't the most pressing need.

But this was a critical design juncture. If not set up properly, the opportunity for reaping the full impact of strategic inquiry could be lost. Deanna said:

> Here's the problem with focusing only on those students. The most important goal in strategic inquiry is to learn something new. What we've been doing is based on what we already know. What we do now leads to current results. So we definitely need to learn something about where exactly your specific kids get stuck.
>
> If you pick only upper-level students, you won't have time to do that. The pressure to move them quickly is just too great. I'm not saying it's not important to move the older kids. You have to do it, and you will. I'm just saying it's not the best use of our time together, the value-added that this process brings. Inquiry can be a place to slow down and learn with colleagues. Where else do you get that in school? And there's one more reason it's worth taking the time to learn something new—it's what we mean when we say that getting small will make a big difference. Once all your teams have figured out something new, we'll put everything you've learned together and figure out a smart way to respond as a school—a small thing that will make a big difference because it's based on something new that you really truly know. That's how big change will happen in your school.

Nate held his ground. He remained insistent that the process should serve the seniors with immediate and pressing needs. But in the next few moments previously quiet voices countered him, saying, "We're always putting out fires, never getting at the underlying issue. Let's do it differently this time."

Nate had given voice to a real need—an urgent one. But Deanna's move of explaining core strategic inquiry principles in a critical moment provided a counterpoint to the pressures that typically drive decisions and allowed other viewpoints to be heard. In the end, the group managed the urgency/capacity building dilemma by deciding that six of the eight SLCs would select students from the ninth and tenth grades and two would work with seniors. An intervention that pushed against the loudest current in the culture and created space for other priorities to be heard allowed for a more sophisticated balancing of the urgency/capacity building dilemma.

Selecting Students Toward the End of the Process

A New Dorp High School team comprised of four tenth grade English and social studies teachers had been focusing on student learning needs in the area of writing for some time. The team had winnowed its focus to "development of ideas" within a paragraph—students' ability to support a controlling idea with logically developed and sequenced detail sentences. They had created a six-point rubric that was aligned to the required state exams in English and social studies that students would take at the end of tenth grade and had implemented strategies and moved most of their target population forward on their rubric.

In May, the team met for their monthly coaching session with Natasha, the strategic inquiry facilitator.[2] They'd been working with her for almost a year, and by this point they knew the drill. They updated her on progress and collectively determined next steps. With little remaining instructional time and anticipating the year-end sharing of progress with strategic inquiry colleagues, they were eager to give their target students one last push. At the start of the session, Keith pulled out a chart of target students' progress, showed it to Natasha, and said, "So, we're happy with our progress. We've moved most of our students at least one full point on the rubric. We'd like to see if we can move them once more before June."

Comments like "we've moved most of our students" signal missed learning opportunities for teachers and, thus, teachable moments.[3] Natasha looked at the chart that indicated movement for all students, noted the word *most* in Keith's comment, and asked the team, "Who didn't move?"

Typically, it takes a team time to understand a comment like this not as criticism but as a reframing of the conversation from summarizing progress to investigating what more can be learned. Eventually the team learns to recognize these kinds of general statements ("most of our students moved" or "60 percent met standard") as masking assumptions that need to be tested, and team members become increasingly able and willing to challenge each other when they hear them and to receive these challenges as opportunities for learning.

This team, however, was not quite there yet. When Natasha asked who did *not* move, Keith gave the team's rationale, explaining, "We had three other students, but they were ELL [English language learners]. They didn't move at all. They clearly needed something different from the rest of the group, and we don't have a lot of time, so we decided to remove them from our target population."

Natasha held the line. "You can't drop those students."

The team was quiet for a moment, and then another team member said, "We don't know what to do with them. We even talked to our assistant principal and the principal, and they said it was okay to drop them. We're making progress with the other kids. We don't have time to do everything, and the ELL teachers focus on those kids. They're in a special program." In fact, what these students had been getting hadn't been working; that's why they should be in the target population.

Having developed a trusting relationship with the school's leadership and knowing that making progress with ELL students was a schoolwide goal, Natasha felt confident that if she explained her reasoning, the administration would support her. So she insisted, "You can't drop those kids." When the team said again that it didn't have time to do everything, she responded, "You can drop everyone else, but not those kids."

Getting teams to a "stuck" place so they can then move through it is a strategic inquiry facilitator's goal; they push the teams to a stuck place, modeling what they hope team members will come to do independently to move beyond it. Once a team has gotten to this place, the facilitator balances pushing and support, helping the team manage anxiety that being up against the edge of what's known brings and reinforcing the notion that being stuck is a prerequisite for learning something new and, therefore, that it represents progress. In this case, Natasha reframed "stuckness" as progress and, to make movement forward manageable, limited the scope of the team's task. She said, "I know it's hard, but where you are is great! You've shone a light on a problem that we all knew was there, but we never saw it so clearly before. Nobody's been able to move those kids. If you can even begin to figure this out, imagine the contribution you'll make to your school! For June, just move these students one step forward."

"But how?" Keith asked. "They didn't even score a 1 on our rubric. Two of them didn't even answer the question. They didn't write anything at all."

"Well," Natasha said, thinking aloud, "if they didn't even score a 1, the rubric isn't specific enough to tell us what they need. You could start with your 1 category and break it down further. Can they read the question? Can they understand what it asks? Or if you're focusing just on writing, what happens when you ask them a question orally? Where exactly is their learning breaking down, and how will you find out?"

Team members looked at Natasha blankly. They were at a loss. "Just learn one more thing about where they are or what they need," she said. "Just one more thing, and present that to us in June."

As an outside consultant, Natasha knew that, without administrative backing, her charge to the team would be hard to enforce. Teams typically met for coaching near the principal's office, so in this case (like some others) Natasha was able to pull principal DeAngelis into the meeting, explain her thinking, and secure her support. DeAngelis offered to help the team in any way, including by setting up a visit to a nearby school with a great reputation for serving ELL students. Later Natasha met with Christine Drucker, the assistant principal and the team's supervisor-mentor. At first Drucker defended her team members' position to protect them from feeling overwhelmed. After hearing that they could drop other students and Natasha's personal plea (the moral imperative of focusing on stuck students: "What if it were your kid?"), Drucker jumped on board as well.

One month later, the team members eagerly presented their inquiry work to a rapt audience of colleagues, telling the story of how they'd gotten unstuck, what they learned, and how, in the end, they hadn't dropped their other students; they were too invested to let them go. They explained how they'd been up against the wall with no idea how to even begin. They assumed that their three ELL target students might not know anything and that, as teachers, they wouldn't be able to move them. After much stumbling, they told their colleagues, they decided to give these three the same prompt and assignment as their other target students, but in their native languages. To their great surprise, all three scored 5 on the writing rubric when they wrote in their native languages.

This was a huge learning experience for the team members. Their assumptions, they realized, had been completely off. At first they'd assumed the students were deficient. They now knew it was their assessments that were off—that better information would shape an entirely different, more targeted (effective) response. Although the three ELL students didn't actually learn more through this team's inquiry process (it was the team that learned about what the students actually knew but what the teachers had not been able to access) and there was tremendous learning and work still to be done to determine how best to move them, the teachers themselves were forever changed. They were eager to lead colleagues to better serve this population and were more effective in drawing on the strategic inquiry design elements to do so, as were others who experienced a similarly dramatic Phase I realization, our research shows. They were less likely to make assumptions about these and other students; and they now understood, they said, how in inquiry "less is more."

Because it was obvious that the team members had pressed through not knowing and gotten to the other side, their colleagues sat on the edge of their seats, captivated during the presentation. This shared experience catalyzed mind shifts for this first cohort of strategic inquiry leaders (thirty teachers and administrators), who in the next two years brought their school culture to a tipping point that continues to pay off today.

This example illustrates how opportunities to push team learning by getting small can arise at any time during the inquiry process and the potential benefit of prioritizing capacity building even in what seems like the final hour. Drucker and others still point to this experience as pivotal in their own development as internal strategic inquiry facilitators who now effectively draw on the strategy of getting small when they as individuals, teams they supervise, or the school as a whole need to learn something new.

HOW SMALL? THE ISSUE OF GRAIN SIZE

Strategic inquiry differs from other versions of inquiry-based reform in its grain size for leveraging change. Most inquiry-based strategies involve drilling down to identify skill gaps. None that we know of requires teams to become as narrowly focused as in strategic inquiry. Teams that seem to understand this idea in theory are surprised by how small they need to get in practice. When school teams are first asked to diagnose and close skill gaps as small as sequencing transitions (*first, next, finally*), for example, or to recognize the commas that surround a noun (appositive) phrase rather than context clues writ large, they question how getting small could possibly move students as quickly or as far as they need to go.

The response of strategic inquiry is, *What's the alternative?* How, if not through more precise diagnostics, will a team and the school learn something new when they are stuck? Of course, the strategy can be misapplied. The key is understanding how getting small works strategically, including when going too small or staying small for too long causes teams to miss the big picture that a sequence of targeted interventions is intended to bring about or the larger system change that getting small should inform.

Strategic inquiry facilitators navigate the small-big dilemma. They guide a team in making decisions about when to get small and how small, when to get big and how big, when and how to draw on available tools. In each case, there is no one right decision or move. Rather, the quality of a team's decisions and moves depends on their being grounded in evidence of evolving student learning needs. The best guiding principle is that a team gets smaller when current knowledge is insufficient for moving students forward—, when more precise diagnostics are needed to inform next steps; therefore, it is worth the time it takes to create and use them (see figure 3.1).

FIGURE 3.1   How small is small enough?

Skill (way too big)	Subskill (still too big— what does it really mean?)	Learning target (just right— I can explain it so everyone can understand, and I can teach it tomorrow)
Expository writing	Coherence	Transitions
Reading comprehension	Context clues	Commas as context clues
Multistep equations	Operations with signed numbers	Adding and subtracting signed numbers

Note: There is no one right size for a learning target. The idea is to get precise information about where learning is breaking down and what exactly needs to be taught. A "just-right" learning target can (when needed) be broken down further into what we call a "tennis chart" (see appendix A).

Why Focus Very Small?

When the strategic inquiry facilitator, Deanna, arrived at Jefferson, SLC leaders had already identified writing as a high-leverage area of focus. Their students weren't meeting the low-bar writing standards required for success in current course work and exams, so how, they wondered, would they ever meet the more rigorous, imminent demands of Common Core State Standards? Improved writing skills, they reasoned, would help students perform better on current and future assessments and in school, work, and life in general.

Most efforts to improve student writing take the high bar as a starting point. They identify the gap between what students currently produce and what they need to produce and then work backward in a kind of common-sense approach, teaching and requiring students to include the most obviously missing elements: evidence, detail, argumentative structures, etc.

Strategic inquiry takes a different approach. The goal is the same: to bring students from where they are to where they need to be. The first step may be the same as well, to identify current reality, an accurate representation of the gap between what they can and need to do. What's different here is the push (modeled by the outside facilitator) for teams to identify extremely granular components of that gap—sentence-level skills—and to stick with a foundational focus for some time. In this case, six subject-area teams in one of Jefferson's SLCs spent their entire first strategic inquiry semester diagnosing and then moving target students in correctly using three conjunctions: *but, because, so.*

This SLC selected ninth graders for their target population and therefore had time and space to do in-depth work on fundamental skills. Deanna reasoned that, with ninth graders rather than upperclassmen, the teachers would be more willing to study something that did not yield an immediate payoff on a summative exam. Her move to push this team to get so small was built on the learning of teams in other schools that had already identified particular skill gaps in writing. The facilitator reasoned she could accelerate the team's progress by focusing its inquiry on these specific skills.

Typically, those seeking to improve student writing are uncomfortable and/or unwilling to focus so narrowly on developing students' foundational writing and reading skills, especially given current pressures to move all students up as fast as possible to a college-ready bar, even in the contained space of an inquiry investigation. What's often misunderstood, however, is that when missing building blocks are identified and put into place, student learning accelerates. This is where the tight focus is strategic; backfilling foundational skills that scaffold complex reasoning and expression is essential if students are to meet the demands of the CCSS.

Deanna led the teacher-leaders in this SLC to this precise focus. First, team leaders identified writing as a focus, collected writing samples for target students in each content area team, and struggled in exploring this student work with their teachers to identify where to begin. When Deanna later asked the leaders what students seem to need most next, the leaders said the students needed almost everything. When Deanna asked, "Like what?" the leaders pulled out student work and their beginning analyses and said, "Well, mechanics, organization, topic sentences, details, and evidence."

Drawing on her knowledge of prior teams that had identified sentence-level strategies as a pressing and typically underdiagnosed and underaddressed need, Deanna asked, "Where do you think the students struggle most—with organizational or sentence-level problems?"

The coleaders, one an English teacher and the other a science teacher, paused and looked at each other. "I never thought about that . . . Probably sentences," the English teacher said hesitantly. The science teacher shrugged.

Deanna told them that she had a tool (designed by another school team) that helps teachers see where students struggle most—with organization, like using a topic sentence and details, or sentence-level skills, like using accurate and varied language or conjunctions to make sentences more complex. They were eager to see the tool, and once she shared it they were off and running (see appendix B). The team leaders developed a common prompt for a new diagnostic paragraph and led their teams in using the tool to analyze results. Each team concluded that sentence-level instruction is what the students needed next. They narrowed their diagnosis further and saw that students struggled most with conjunctions. In response, they created a more finely broken down "tennis chart" (see appendix C and figures 3.2 and 3.3) to capture each student's ability and group patterns in understanding *but, because, so*. This tool, essential for guiding teams to articulate and track progress on the smaller components of a larger skill, is called a "tennis chart" (rather than a learning progression or task analysis) to indicate that the skills listed are not necessarily comprehensive or linear; they are akin to the smaller skills a tennis player might draw on in mastering the serve (foot position, ball toss, grip). A player might master one or more skills but be missing a fundamental element. Similarly, target students may be missing one or more (but not all) prerequisites or foundational elements of a larger skill.[4]

Although conjunctions may seem like a ridiculously narrow focus, tenuous buy-in was more fully realized when teachers saw that in fact their focal students did not use *but, because, so* correctly and that definitions which at first appeared simple were less simple and more critical for students to master than they originally thought. For example, *but* signals a change in direction that is qualified rather than complete; *so* is the crux of cause and effect. These teams stayed with conjunctions for a semester not because they set out to do so but because the ongoing, investigative process of identifying and clearly defining the skill gaps, developing strategies across content areas to address them, diagnosing movement and remaining gaps, and adjusting strategies in ongoing evidence-based cycles of action research took time.

This narrow focus on specific learning targets was critical in making manageable what was otherwise overwhelming. The team moved smoothly into sharing accountability for moving struggling students forward and for learning new strategies with one another. Focusing on one essential skill (conjunctions) that was relevant across subjects was strategic in moving high school teachers from seeing themselves strictly as content teachers to ensuring that time spent on literacy supported, rather than took away from, content-specific instructional goals. The common focus pushed instructional coherence; teachers began using common literacy strategies in the service of varied instructional goals (math content could be supported by use of conjunctions as easily as in social studies, for example) and supported skill-based differentiation across classrooms (one

FIGURE 3.2   Tracking mastery of sentence skills

	Expanding sentences (with who, where, how, when, why)	Providing examples	Using transitions	Using conjunctions
Student 1	N	N	N	N
Student 2	N	Y	N	N
Student 3	Y	Y	N	N
Student 4	Y	Y	Y	N
Student 5	Y	Y	N	N
Student 6	N	Y	N	N
Student 7	Y	Y	Y	Y
Student 8	Y	Y	N	N
Student 9	N	N	N	N
Student 10	Y	Y	N	N

FIGURE 3.3   Tracking mastery of conjunctions

	But		Because		So	
	outside content	with content	outside content	with content	outside content	with content
Student 1	Y	Y	Y	N	Y	N
Student 2	Y	N	Y	N	Y	N
Student 3	Y	Y	Y	Y	N	N
Student 4	Y	Y	Y	Y	Y	Y
Student 5	Y	Y	Y	Y	N	N
Student 6	Y	Y	Y	N	N	N
Student 7	N	N	Y	N	N	N
Student 8	Y	Y	Y	Y	N	N
Student 9	Y	Y	N	N	Y	N
Student 10	Y	Y	Y	N	Y	Y

student could use *but, because, so* while another used the more complex "hinge" words, *however, since, therefore*).

Getting small mattered for students across subjects in this case because conjunctions supported students' learning of specific instructional goals. In math, students' knowledge was tested and reinforced when they wrote sentences such as "Correlation does not imply causation, but causation does imply correlation." In science, students' knowledge was tested and reinforced when they wrote sentences such as: "Starches are considered carbohydrates because they produce energy." Getting small with a focus on conjunctions was a worthy investment for two other reasons as well. First, it supported teachers in learning to diagnose and successfully address student skill gaps. Second, multiple teams aggregated their findings, identified patterns, and positioned themselves to select and implement an instructional change schoolwide.

Strategic inquiry requires that a teacher team focus closely on those areas in which they have hit the limits of what they know. The Phase I design, along with strategic facilitation, forces the team to push through discomfort until they learn something new. What's most uncomfortable is that the current culture of schooling positions teachers as experts who implement best practices rather than as inquirers who become experts in continuous learning. Once team members move through their initial frustration or experience of feeling decentered, however, and learn something new together, many are thrilled by the experience. Some teachers have commented that doing so reignites the passion that initially drew them to teaching.

Most essential in Phase I is that teams come to develop a basic understanding of the strategic inquiry process, especially the fundamental importance of getting small to achieve student gains and the norm of public learning and shared accountability. Having learned from a facilitator's modeling, they are ready to ask hard questions of themselves and to apply core inquiry strategies for moving students and colleagues in the next two phases.

CHAPTER 4

Moving Instructional Systems to Improve Success

Although a team can make big improvements for struggling students by addressing their particular learning needs, instructional conditions in the school can work systematically against the students' progress. In Phase II, teams shine the light that was on target students onto themselves and the schoolwide learning conditions that constrain student success. They interrogate the routines and practices that constitute business as usual and are not typically subject to scrutiny. They come to understand how common assumptions about teaching and learning result in particular decisions that limit student success. Once they see how this works in their school, they can identify what needs to change and take action.

The lynchpin for a team's success in moving a system is the precise skill gap identified in Phase I. Analysis of current conditions through this lens illuminates what exactly needs to change, and closing this gap is the marker of improvement. Strategic inquiry highlights and defines four instructional subsystems, or areas, in which decisions largely determine the conditions under which students learn:

- What is taught (curriculum)
- Who teaches (teacher assignment)

- How teaching occurs (lesson design and pedagogy)
- How well teaching occurs (supervisory focus and professional learning opportunities).

In analyzing each subsystem through the lens of the identified skill gap, a team comes to a crystal-clear understanding of how current practices produce student underperformance and how decisions in each area are typically made—what people do and do not pay attention to, the more or less conscious and/or public factors that result in decisions to implement those practices. Teams are led to focus on and to improve one subsystem at a time. This makes the work manageable and ensures particular shifts in that area (see figure 4.1).

Focusing on one subsystem at a time is strategic in that each is a microcosm of the whole instructional system. Strategic inquiry separates the subsystems for analysis, but in practice they are interrelated, and changed decision making within one subsystem spills over into others.

FIGURE 4.1   What drives decision making in instructional subsystems? Phase II shifts

Instructional subsystem	From decisions based on . . .	To decisions based on . . .
What is taught (curriculum)	Content on curriculum map and pacing guides	Student learning gaps (content and skills)
How teaching occurs (lesson design and pedagogy)	Best practices (as decided by district or school)	Evidence of what closes learning gaps
Who teaches (teacher assignment)	Teachers with seniority get "best"/older students	Students with priority needs get teachers best prepared to address them
How well teaching occurs (supervisory focus and professional learning opportunities)	Supervisory/professional development focus based on criteria for best practice	Supervisory/professional development focus based on identified student learning needs and corresponding teacher learning needs

CHALLENGES TO MOVING A SYSTEM

Core challenges a teacher team undertakes during this phase that are most important for success include:

- Seeing school learning conditions through the lens of struggling students

- Selecting one high-leverage instructional subsystem to analyze, improve, and track improvements within (the one in which change will yield the biggest difference for students)

- Designing a change strategy that builds on and is aligned with established routines

- Taking action to shift ideas about leadership and develop change leaders

- Deepening inquiry as a habit of mind.

The design of strategic inquiry—its tasks, tools, and strategic facilitation—supports a team in navigating these challenges. Team members deepen their understanding and skills by repeating the inquiry process and applying the core principles they used to move students to system-level problems.

SEEING INSTRUCTIONAL SYSTEMS THROUGH THE LENS OF STUDENT SKILL GAPS

A main inhibitor of a school's ongoing improvement is teachers' and administrators' focus on teaching rather than learning. Conceptualizing teacher effectiveness in terms of following a curriculum or using particular teaching strategies provides no check on what constitutes improvement. Teachers might seem to be improving without any evidence that what they are doing actually works for struggling students.

Strategic inquiry directly targets this cultural constraint on improving student achievement. It prompts a team to interrogate how school decisions keep some students out of the sphere of success, and, in doing so, to come face-to-face with the immediate impact of these decisions. By analyzing instructional practices through the lens of an identified skill gap, the team members shift their focus from delivering a curriculum to its impact. Before this analysis they might say, "We taught it, but they didn't learn." After they are more likely to say, "Students needed it, and it wasn't taught."

One tool that helps teacher teams make this shift is low inference transcripts. A LIT is a verbatim transcription of a class—just the facts, what teachers and students do and say with as little judgment as possible (see appendix A).[1] It takes a bit of practice to develop the LIT muscle, to capture what happens in a class quickly and accurately enough to produce a trustworthy transcript, one that the observed teacher would see as accurate, unbiased, and fair. Yet learning to create the transcripts shifts team members' focus from teaching to student learning. As one strategic inquiry team member explained after completing only two LITs, "I used to just look at the teacher at the front of the room. Now when I observe, I look at what she's doing, but I pay more attention to how what she's doing is landing on the kids."

But it's the analysis of multiple classroom transcripts through the lens of student skill gaps that brings about the biggest shifts. Absent the focus on a particular skill gap, flaws in the system will not necessarily become apparent. For example, one team was focused on student weaknesses in the area of writing. When asked to analyze schoolwide instructional practices related to writing, such as what exactly is taught, how it's taught, and how decisions about teacher assignment, professional learning opportunities, and/or supervisory focus impact student ability in this area, their answers were not particularly helpful in isolating a cause for writing problems or a solution. Team members said, "Yes, we teach writing. There's been a big push from administration this year to incorporate it as much as possible. In English and social studies, most teachers start each class with a DO NOW that requires writing. My supervisor always looks for that when he observes. He wants to see that kids have an opportunity to write every day."

Analyzing these same practices through the lens of a more specific skill gap, however, revealed the causes of the gap. The team looked more deeply into writing problems and realized that its target students could not logically sequence their written ideas. To determine why students lacked this skill, the team members analyzed the curriculum as taught and captured in the LITs. They read through twenty-five ninth grade English and social studies transcripts and counted the number of times students were taught or provided an opportunity to practice the identified skill. The number was zero. Of course, it's possible that the skill was taught in classes not captured by these specific transcripts, but the goal was to present a convincing, not an iron-clad, case. When other school leaders asked if these transcripts seemed representative, the group said "yes." Next, the team examined teacher assignments and discovered a long-standing pattern: the most experienced teachers were assigned to the oldest and most successful students. Then members looked at lesson design and pedagogy. A change to these areas alone, they came to realize, would never result in target students getting what they had been found to need. A teacher could use more group work or student-led discussion, but without inserting "sequencing ideas in writing" into the curriculum in some form, students were unlikely to learn it. Even the supervisory focus on daily writing, they came to understand, was too general to ensure its desired effect.

The awareness they gained from analyzing practices in terms of a precise student skill gap was huge—and often devastating to team members. "I use those DO NOWs at the beginning of the period," one teacher confessed. "I used to think I was teaching writing. But when I looked at all those transcripts, I saw the pattern. We're having kids write, but we're not *teaching* writing. And that's why they can't do it!"

By implication, the effectiveness of a system change is directly related to the quality of a team's diagnosis of specific student learning needs in Phase I. If the diagnosis is too general, the change is likely to miss the mark, as evidenced in the school where "DO NOWs" had been implemented. In another NYC high school we'll call Nautilus, a change was initiated prematurely, before a team's Phase I inquiry was complete. The mathematics team had identified academic vocabulary as the problem area early in its Phase I work. As their inquiry to move students continued, team members shared emerging findings with the math assistant principal, who was not a part of the team, and she jumped the gun to create a department-level response. She worked with her department to identify key academic vocabulary needed in various math courses and then to incorporate the terms into common midterm and final exams. Since the team was still focused on moving target students, it did not track the results of the system response that its work had prompted prematurely. But the vagueness of this new policy limited its potential to impact teaching and learning.

One month later, the math team's Phase I work was deeper and more focused. The team had homed in more tightly and realized that it wasn't just vocabulary in general that was the problem. Members focused on one particularly problematic word, *slope,* and created a highly scaffolded assessment breaking down what a student would have to know and be able to do to understand and use the concept. They discovered that "vocabulary" was too general a diagnosis to address the root of the problem. In fact, the team's target students did not know the difference between the Y and the X axis or how to plot data points and were confused about the difference between the X axis and the X in algebra (the unknown). The team was prepared at this point to design and initiate a system response that would target and respond to a more precise understanding of the underlying deficit than the assistant principal's response, which focused on math course vocabulary. Its next step was to work with the math assistant principal to institute foundational skill-based diagnostics for incoming students. They could no longer make assumptions, team members realized, about what each student knew and didn't know when they entered the ninth grade.

SELECTING THE HIGHEST-PRIORITY INSTRUCTIONAL SUBSYSTEM TO IMPROVE

Once team members see school conditions through struggling students' eyes and the cause-effect relationship between teacher decisions and student results, they are well positioned and eager to push change. To make this work manageable, strategic inquiry directs teams to improve one instructional subsystem at a time. First, they select the subsystem that can make the biggest difference, and almost every strategic inquiry team across cohorts, school levels, and iterations of the program selects curriculum. Almost every team found that the identified skill gap exists because it is not taught.

At Jefferson High School, for example, multiple teams identified sentence-level foundational skill deficits in their Phase I work. Over the course of inquiry into student learning deficits and what strategies worked to move those students between October and January, ten teacher teams across four SLCs found that students struggled with using conjunctions to link ideas within sentences and transition words to bring coherence to ideas within a paragraph, as well as other foundational skills. To close these gaps, the teams adopted a set of effective strategies from a program used by a neighboring school. After aggregating what was learned across the multiple teams, they decided to continue their inquiry into identifying and closing foundational gaps in writing the following semester, and they decided to simultaneously design and begin preparation for a system change that would respond to what they'd learned. Between February and June, curriculum development teams formed to create materials so that the school could launch a ninth grade basic skills writing program in English, math, social studies, science, and physical education classes the following September.

Jefferson benefited from the work of prior teams in that the outside facilitator, drawing on tools developed via inquiry across other schools, was able to accelerate their work, leading them to see certain deficits more rapidly than prior teams had done and pointing them to a system response (in this case, a specific writing program that addressed these particular gaps). The teams' discovery that what students outside the sphere of success lacked were fundamental literacy skills—skills so fundamental, in many cases, that they would never have even thought to test knowledge of them—was consistent with what almost every strategic inquiry–based team has found.

IDENTIFYING A LEVERAGE POINT FOR SYSTEM CHANGE CONNECTED TO SKILL GAPS

Once teacher teams have selected which instructional subsystem they will improve, they must come to understand how decisions in the subsystem are typically made so that they are able to best alter and improve those decisions. They typically find that decisions about what to teach are driven by external factors rather than by students' needs. Typically, teachers face pressure to teach to an external standard, curriculum map, and/or summative exam and are pushed to cover and rush through a curriculum rather than to adjust that curriculum in response to what the students know and need. Where decisions about what to teach are based on evidence of student knowledge, this is often in response to the "average" student. How, teachers wonder, could they design a class with the most struggling students' needs as the driver of decisions when there is such pressure to raise all students to an increasingly higher standard?

The inquiry team's job, then, is to align decisions in one instructional subsystem—again, most often curriculum—more closely with evidence of struggling students' need. In order to make this happen, teams are led to understand how current decisions about what to teach (that result in identified skill gaps) are typically made: what and/or who is a teacher typically paying attention to and responding to when she makes decisions about what exactly to teach? Although the general problem, that these decisions are not based on struggling students' needs, is similar across schools represented by strategic inquiry teams, the manifestation of those problems is particular to a context. In order to leverage change that addresses the skill gaps of struggling students, a team needs to look closely at the key players, values, underlying assumptions, habits, etc., that guide decision making in their particular environment. Once they have a clear understanding of what and who people in their school do (and do not) pay attention to, they are equipped to design a lever for change that could make a big difference in their particular school.

This is no small challenge. Teachers steeped in the culture of their own school may not see what is taken for granted, and most have little or no experience thinking about organizations as systems or how to use power relations and routines to bring about change in the way people do things. One team, for example, clearly identified what it wanted to change but struggled to understand how best to effect this change in its school environment. The team had evidence from its Phase I inquiry that a focus on five high-leverage academic terms in each unit in the Global History course led to a big boost in target students' performance, that a focus on these explicit terms and concepts was a small change that made a big difference. The team's desired system change, then, was to ensure that all teachers of this course would focus on these identified words.

However, its first strategy was unsuccessful. Trying to use what already existed in the environment, team members decided to piggyback on a recent administrative mandate that required teachers to post key academic terms on their classroom walls. The team worked with the assistant principal of social studies to adjust the mandate so that the high-leverage terms were required for these Word Walls. When they tracked the impact of this strategy, however, team members found that it did not improve student performance. They found that even though teachers complied by putting words on the wall, they did not necessarily emphasize or teach those words; nor did students pay much attention to them. This is where failed improvement efforts often go wrong: change leaders conflate what's supposed to drive teacher behavior with what actually drives it.

The team's second intervention was more effective because it was based on a clearer understanding of what teachers in this department did pay attention to in deciding what to teach. The team members focused on common, unit-based formative assessments created by the assistant principal that were mapped to the year-end summative assessment and intended to provide regular information about student progress and resulting teacher needs. At monthly department meetings, teachers were asked to share assessment results and identify where students struggled. The team's second idea was to insert the five selected terms into each unit's common assessment. Because team members presented powerful evidence of the strategy having worked with other students, the assistant principal agreed to the experiment. The strategy paid off in June in improved student performance on the Global Studies Regents exam (which is the "gatekeeper" in New York, with the highest proportions of students not graduating due to failing this exam). The key to its success was pushing particular high-leverage words in a way that capitalized on what teachers already paid attention to.

Although strategic, this system change was just one step toward the ultimate goal of a true system change, one in which evidence is routinely used for continuous improvement. In strategic inquiry, teams determine the best next step for improving systems to address student skill gaps.

DEVELOPING AN IDENTITY AS A LEADER

The design of strategic inquiry for system change challenges team members' belief that only those with positional power can lead change. It pushes them to take action and to develop a sense of themselves as leaders by doing so regardless of formal position. The strategic inquiry stance is that everyone has the ability and the responsibility to lead change—and that you work with whatever you've got to do so. Progress is defined as pushing improvement forward.

As in other phases, core tasks, tools, and strategic facilitation push teacher learning through action, prompting team practices that produce results and shift beliefs in reinforcing cycles. By initiating school change without positional authority, team members come to see themselves as change leaders, and then to see their colleagues and students as allies in improvement efforts. Along the way, they inevitably both encounter resistance from and win over their colleagues using evidence. Christine, a teacher in a small high school in the Bronx who was pursuing administrative positions at the time of our interview, put it this way:

> If we'd only designed an intervention for those twenty [target students], then you wouldn't have had the experience of implementing a schoolwide initiative and working with a lot of teachers. You would have had a very small group who in theory wanted to work with you, and I wouldn't have necessarily had the experience of working with somebody who was opposed to my plan . . . We pushed back with: "These twenty represent the problems that most of our students have . . . So if these twenty can't make a graph, probably 80 percent of our five hundred can't make a graph. So let's do it for everyone."

The system changes accomplished by members of a New Dorp High School team with varying levels of positional authority illustrate the idea that everyone can push change in the best ways available given their current position. This team was comprised of two teacher-leaders and an assistant principal of mathematics. Early in its Phase I work, the team discovered that students struggled with fractions, something they were already expected to know and that teachers infrequently taught. As soon as this became clear, Li Pan, the assistant principal, responded by changing what teachers did together at regular department meetings. He realized that his teachers felt compelled to teach to a given pacing calendar (which was mapped to a high-stakes year-end exam) and that they didn't feel it was acceptable to stop or to slow down, even when students were falling behind. Pan decided to use department meeting time to have teachers examine the results of frequent skill-based assessments and, in response, to collectively adjust the pacing calendar.

Concurrently, the team investigated how practices in multiple instructional systems collectively created the skill gap. This prompted the math teacher on the team to initiate a change related to teacher assignment that required no formal authority and that caught on across the building, resulting in improvement in various subjects and sectors. Seeing clearly the collective impact of the newest, least-experienced teachers being assigned to the youngest and most struggling students, Dara Lapkin, an experienced teacher-leader, asked to be assigned to teach the weakest ninth grade students the following year and to loop with those students, keeping them until the end of tenth grade, the year of their high-stakes summative exam.[2] Teacher-leaders in the other seven strategic inquiry teams recognized a similar phenomenon and its collective impact on the students they studied and also asked to teach ninth grade the following year.

This system change (along with others happening as a result of a series of revelations that studying target populations brings) made a huge difference in the progress of the following year's cohort of students. Lapkin raised her entire class of students, all of whom had entered way below grade level on the eighth grade math exams, to pass the required high-stakes state exam one semester early the following year—before she left for maternity leave. The shift in culture that led other experienced teachers to want to focus on this same class had a lasting impact on this cohort; their graduation rates soared. This resulted, ironically, in a lesson in unintended consequences. The shift of experienced teachers to the ninth grade left the tenth grade at a disadvantage, one that this student cohort was never able to entirely overcome.

Reflecting on this early experience, New Dorp principal Deirdre De-Angelis emphasized that learning to create adaptable systems involves a big learning curve: "We were really unsophisticated then." Later, New Dorp teams learned to adapt to student need while embedding feedback loops and seeing consequences in other areas early enough to make ongoing adjustments. The primary point here is that a system change that made a big difference in student performance was initiated by teachers who saw the impact of their own decision making on specific students. This change worked, DeAngelis maintained, because it grew from the ground up rather than being mandated from above. The idea of teacher seniority and choice was so deeply engrained in school culture that it took teacher leadership and leading by example to shift it. A top-down mandate probably would have generated unnecessary resentment or resistance to a change that, when led by teachers, was seamless.

APPLYING AN ONGOING INQUIRY PROCESS

The strategic inquiry design for continuous progress challenges teams to apply the same skills they used to move students forward through inquiry to move their school systems forward. Once teams identify what exactly they want to change in a system and how they will act to change it, the most challenging work involves responding to the difference between what they expect to happen as they implement their change strategy and what actually happens. Like all change efforts, the hardest Phase II work is making strategic adjustments in response to real-time evidence.

Most important is having a clear driving hypothesis ("We believe that if we do X, it will lead to Y") as well as aligned benchmarks and evidence to inform continual adjustments in a strategy along the way. Determining benchmarks is trickier than it sounds, because the evidence necessary is different from what team members have learned to collect in Phase I.

The earlier example of an intervention to change department meetings illustrates rigorous inquiry. The hypothesis was, "We believe that if we change the focus of department meetings to adjusting the pacing calendar in response to our analysis of ongoing assessments, teaching practice will become more skill based and aligned with evidence of student needs." Testing this hypothesis, or measuring the effectiveness of the system change, involved:

- Determining a measurable baseline for both student performance and teacher practice

- Collecting evidence of the actual change to see if it is implemented as intended

- Identifying benchmarks of progress, interim evidence to indicate changes in practice and student knowledge in alignment with the theory of change embedded in the hypothesis

- Determining a measurable goal for teacher practices and student performance.

The challenge is designing a clear, measurable end goal that is linked to student performance and clear aligned benchmarks for tracking progress. In this instance, the assistant principal tracked improvements in ninth grade performance on common unit assessments. For benchmarks, he tracked what happened at meetings (what interim assessments revealed about student learning gaps and what the teachers discussed in terms of practice in relation to those gaps) and evidence from classroom observations that teachers revisited skills and topics as needed, even when doing so put them out of sync with the state pacing calendar.

Every system change doesn't need to be tracked with this level of detail. But in learning to articulate and to track key elements of a tight hypothesis that directly responds to and is measured against closing students' skill gaps, team members develop the *strategic inquiry reflex*—the habit of mind of going small to go big and of adjusting decisions in response to evidence that is tightly aligned to their cause-effect hypothesis.

When coming to the end of an intensive inquiry cycle, teams often express relief, sometimes in joking terms: now that they've moved a system, finally the hard work is over.

Engaging in the model's inquiry process—going small to go big—does get easier and more rewarding as team members and a larger number of colleagues internalize the knowledge and skills needed to use it well. But it is never easy.

The strategic inquiry design for system change, particularly the importance of getting small, plays the greatest role in guiding team success. The facilitator holds teams to the design, ensuring that they analyze school conditions in light of the precise learning gap identified in Phase I and that they test the emerging plan for change in light of its potential to close that very gap. The facilitator helps teams use available systems tools—schema for understanding interrelationship of parts within a larger system, for instance, and for mapping the interconnections and seeing alternatives and/or potential areas of change. In the process of learning to move the system in a specific way that addresses a particular student learning gap, team members come to see their school differently and themselves as change leaders.

CHAPTER 5

Moving Colleagues Toward
a School Inquiry Culture

In the first two phases of strategic inquiry, a school team improves student learning and school practices without necessarily teaching others the inquiry skills and habits that allowed them to do so. The team improves instruction for struggling students by changing the information available to teachers, for example, rather than by developing colleagues' ability to identify and strategically remove inhibitors of student success. In this third phase, team members increase the number of teachers who know and can apply the strategic inquiry reflex.

Schools that have gone beyond the tipping point to develop a robust inquiry culture across the faculty did so by developing inquiry leadership over a period of roughly three years. Over time these schools not only involved all teachers in well-led inquiry teams but created and revised systems and tools to support and systematize the work.

The schools we studied that reached this point used various approaches to developing leadership to spread and deepen strategic inquiry in the school. In one, an initial cohort of teacher teams took on the role of leading inquiry with a new cohort of teams; in another, successive teacher cohorts completed the credentialing program and led inquiry teams across the school; in two others, trained facilitators used strategic inquiry as the core improvement strategy in turnaround schools.

Regardless of the school's scaling-up strategy, those who step into the role of inquiry leader face several key challenges:

- Deciding how to move forward given particulars of their context (how to stage and organize the shift and what to hold tight versus loose)

- Navigating resistance

- Applying strategic inquiry principles and processes to moving adults as well as students.

As in earlier phases of developing strategic inquiry skills, a facilitator supports team members as they grapple with these challenges and ideally works with the school principal and/or administrative team to codesign the change process. Team members faced with the task of moving colleagues typically encounter the same frustrations they encountered when they initially took on the task of moving struggling students, such as the challenges of crafting precise, measurable learning goals and learning from evidence to decide next steps. A facilitator can remind them of what they learned about navigating the challenges in earlier phases, and, in being reminded, they more quickly learn to adapt the same skills and processes to moving adults than it took them to learn the skills initially. Once they see the connections among the three phases and see how strategic inquiry works similarly, differently, and synergistically in all three, they are ready to take on the role of strategic inquiry facilitator in any school.

To show how the change process unfolds over time, we tell the story of a large NYC high school that has made dramatic progress through strategic inquiry—how school administrators and an outside facilitator staged the development of inquiry leadership, how the substance of inquiry evolved, and how inquiry became institutionalized.

TURNING AROUND A LARGE HIGH SCHOOL THROUGH STRATEGIC INQUIRY

In 2006, the principal and cabinet at New Dorp High School, partnered with Natasha, a strategic inquiry facilitator, to support instructional improvement during a floor-to-ceiling redesign of the school into eight theme-based smaller learning communities. Since becoming principal eight years earlier, DeAngelis had led the school in steady improvement; however, she and her administrative team had hit a wall. SLCs, they believed, would create the needed personalized environment for students, but structural change alone, they knew, was insufficient for bringing about the needed improvement.

In January 2006, DeAngelis led thirty administrators and teacher-leaders (later named Cohort 1) in taking the leap of faith required to invest in learning and applying strategic inquiry at the very same time they were creating new SLCs to launch the following September. Over the next three years—and continuing to this day in ways that neither New Dorp leaders nor strategic inquiry designers could have anticipated at the time—this investment deepened and spread, yielding such steady increases in student achievement and shifts in school culture that, after three years, the culture had tipped to one of broadly distributed leadership for continous, evidence-based improvement. Indicators of New Dorp's stunning success include improved

- Graduation rates: Rose from 54.9 percent in 2005 to 75.8 percent in 2011

- Attendance: Rose from 88 percent in 2005 to 92 percent in 2012[1]

- NYC Progress Report Grade: Rose from a low C in 2005 to an A in 2010 and 2011 and a high B in 2012

- Quality Review Rating:[2] Improved from "proficient" in the first year to "well-developed," the highest possible score, each year thereafter

- State standing: Went from being a "school in need of improvement" to meeting "safe harbor," to being a school "in good standing" in 2012.

New Dorp's ability to reap such dramatic benefits from strategic inquiry lies in the quality of strategic decision making by school leaders in partnership with a skilled facilitator at every stage of implementation and development, including about how best to structure and roll out inquiry, to respond to the substance of what was being learned, and to systematize its core strategies and principles schoolwide.

STAGING THE DEVELOPMENT OF INQUIRY LEADERSHIP

Principal DeAngelis's first strategic decision was her design for leadership. She and her cabinet determined that each SLC would be led by a subject-area assistant principal along with two teacher-leaders, a dedicated guidance counselor, and a school aide. This cross-hatching (leadership by a subject-area supervisor and teachers from across subjects, together responsible for improving student performance within their content area and across areas for the students in their SLC) would, DeAngelis and her cabinet imagined, have a synergistic effect.

In addition, DeAngelis was strategic in how she constituted the teams and structured their work. First, she selected teachers who volunteered before knowing they would be paid for their involvement. "I wanted people who wanted to be part of change for change's sake," she explained. Second, she involved the assistant principals, who already had administrator certification and therefore elected not to participate in the credentialing version of strategic inquiry. She explained, "Since what we learned was going to be so critical for how our school moved forward, I wanted everyone learning strategic inquiry to be together on a level playing field." Third, and most important, she prioritized time for instructional improvement during the redesign. She secured an agreement from all members of Cohort 1 (SLC leaders and other key administrators) to meet for three hours weekly after school with Natasha, the outside facilitator, to engage in the strategic inquiry process.

Early on the outside facilitator partnered with the principal and her cabinet in addressing resistance, and their strategic, unified response was critical in establishing the principal's commitment to instructional improvement and authorizing the facilitator's work. As part of strategic inquiry's design at New Dorp, Natasha met monthly with each teacher-leader for individual coaching. During the second coaching visit, about one month into strategic inquiry implementation, Natasha was confronted with tremendous resistance to using the precious three hours of afterschool meeting time to focus on inquiry. In their individual coaching sessions, one teacher-leader after another said, in essence, "Studying kids is a luxury we don't have right now. We have to teach our regular classes AND create everything about our new SLC from scratch: our identity, activities, structure, policies, electives. We need that three hours every week to build our SLCs."

Given the consistency and strength of the views expressed, and that teachers were not part of a credit-bearing program (as staff at other large high schools were at the time), Natasha knew it would be difficult, if not impossible, to push strategic inquiry forward effectively without administrative support. She was scheduled to lead a three-hour session that afternoon, so she went directly to the principal's office to share what she'd heard and to collectively determine the next steps. Natasha wondered if it was too much to ask; perhaps strategic inquiry was not the best improvement model for a school that was restructuring.

Immediately after hearing Natasha's report, however, DeAngelis and key cabinet members who were present understood this moment as a critical juncture and jumped into action to lead their cadre of new leaders through the process. They set about selecting data to share that afternoon and determining how best to display it. They wanted to make clear to everyone what they knew to be true: not only was the school failing large numbers of students, but the fate of the school itself and of large high schools generally in New York City, it seemed, was at stake. They knew that large high schools were being closed and the buildings used to house multiple smaller high schools throughout the city, and New Dorp's four separate wings would easily accommodate small schools. They knew that there had been improvement, but not enough to stave off closure, they worried. Plus, DeAngelis had been a special education teacher and leader of a model special education program in her previous job. She knew from experience that New Dorp students' failure was not inevitable, as many of her staff seemed to believe, and that if teachers got better at meeting their needs, students would improve.

Two hours later, DeAngelis presented the brutal facts to Cohort 1: "Structural change isn't good enough. If we don't improve our instruction, nothing else we do will matter."From that moment on, everyone knew the stakes involved. They never again voiced doubt about using the three-hour time block for strategic inquiry.

Then the harder work began as they struggled to identify skill gaps, improve practices, and look closely and honestly at themselves. One of the biggest challenges was learning to give and accept honest, specific feedback—coming to see it as appropriate and desirable to push each other to improve. By the end of one semester of strategic inquiry, a new culture was taking root in Cohort 1. They were solidifying a new common language and skills and a reorientation to students and to the strategic inquiry process of digging deeply and pushing each other to continuously improve.

By the following September, teachers across the school were curious about what was going on in those seemingly secret afterschool sessions. Realizing that an "us-them" division was brewing, the principal responded strategically by asking for an additional team of volunteers from each SLC for Cohort 2, which she launched the following January. Natasha continued leading Cohort 1 after school and trained Cohort 2 together with volunteers from Cohort 1. By this point, Cohort 1 leaders had achieved an understanding of and buy-in to the strategic inquiry model and were beginning to see its impact in their own classrooms and beyond. Many said this had been the best professional development they'd had in their careers. For this reason, and because they were struggling to fill the new daily common planning time with something worthwhile (even "kid talk" was devolving into complaining sessions), they decided to turn-key the strategic inquiry model during common planning time schoolwide.

In September 2008, New Dorp launched strategic inquiry across the building as its primary school-improvement strategy. In their afterschool sessions, Cohort 1 leaders prepared for the rollout strategically. They discussed each teacher—who was likely to buy in and who was likely to resist, which resistors could be brought along and by whom, which teachers should be separated so as not to influence each other negatively, which teacher-leaders should be placed where, and so on.

While Cohort 1 leaders enacted all strategic inquiry phases (moving students, moving systems and moving colleagues), the design for schoolwide inquiry involved SLC teams in Phase I (moving students) only, with teacher-leaders and other administrators responsible for Phases II and III. Natasha's role was now to support Cohort 1 leaders in applying strategic inquiry to moving adults—essentially, to develop a cadre of internal facilitators. (Phase III constitutes facilitator training in this sense.) Phase III benchmarks and goals are related to adult learning. They include evidence from LITs of shifts in the quality and nature of teacher talk during inquiry meetings, for example, and of the close tracking, analysis, and honing of their own leadership moves that facilitate these shifts. (See figures 5.1–5.3 for examples from a different school of the shifts inquiry leaders may track and how they demonstrate movement. See appendix D for a rubric that strategic inquiry leaders/facilitators can use to diagnose baseline performance and progress for school teams.)

By the end of year three, New Dorp's culture had changed. In the first year it was not unusual to hear teachers complaining about and/or blaming students. By year three, teams were talking about evidence of learning

FIGURE 5.1   Culture shifts in common planning time: an illustration from one school

Fall	Spring
Most teachers view common planning time as a time to grade papers.	Only two teachers still bring piles of grading to common planning time meetings.
Any off-topic comment derails inquiry work.	Teachers who make off-topic comments are usually ignored.
At least one teacher per meeting goes on a rant about difficulties with students or administration.	There is general frustration with the current school climate; however, rants are few and far between.
Attempts at pushing writing-based inquiry are met with resistance; teachers do not see value, and one teacher's negative comment may spark an entire period's disruption.	Teachers enjoy seeing progress in our inquiry into writing skill gaps, especially in unelaborated paragraphs. Resistant teachers comments are generally ignored.
Inquiry leaders are seen as powerful supervisors dictating what should be done.	Inquiry leaders are accepted as peer leaders, working collaboratively to move students forward.

FIGURE 5.2 Rating growth in teacher buy-in for strategic inquiry

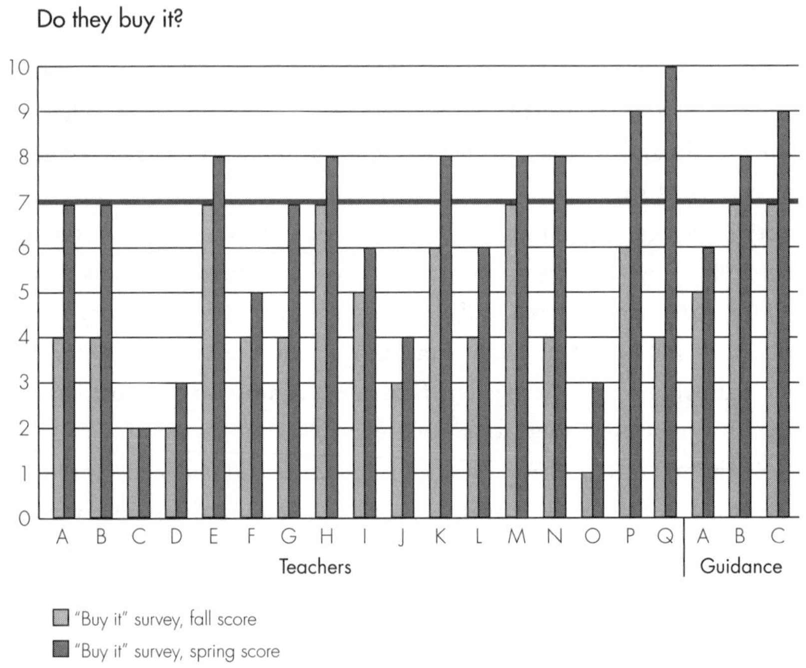
Do they buy it?
10
9
8
7
6
5
4
3
2
1
0
A B C D E F G H I J K L M N O P Q
Teachers
A B C
Guidance
"Buy it" survey, fall score
"Buy it" survey, spring score

Note: The ratings in this figure are based on the scores that inquiry leaders gave to each of the teachers they were working with. The scale was 1–10, with 1 the lowest and 10 the highest; a rating of 7 was considered to be "meeting standard."

gaps and what worked or didn't work to close them. In year one a negative comment about students or the inquiry process was likely to prompt a cascade of negativity. By year three, dissenters were a distinct minority and negative comments were ignored or challenged. By this third year, new teachers entered seamlessly into a new notion of what it meant to work at New Dorp: part of the job was teaching students; equally important was working with colleagues to study and improve teaching practices in light of student skill gaps.

Each SLC leadership team divided up the work of leading inquiry differently. In some SLCs the administrative and teacher-leaders planned and led common planning time together. In others teacher-leaders took charge.

FIGURE 5.3   Rating growth in teacher understanding of strategic inquiry

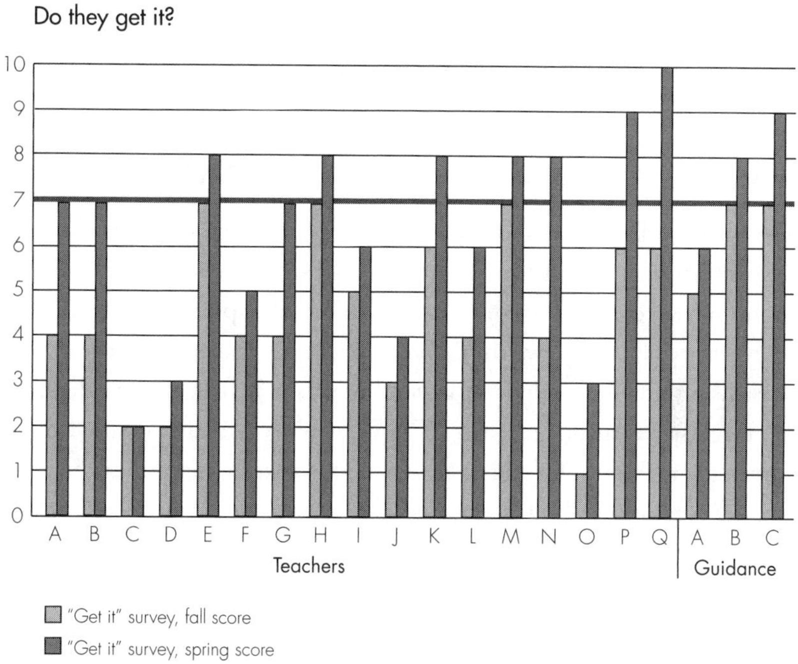

Do they get it?

Note: The ratings in this figure are based on the scores that inquiry leaders gave to each of the teachers they were working with. The scale was 1–10, with 1 the lowest and 10 the highest; a rating of 7 was considered to be "meeting standard."

In one the leadership triad (an assistant principal and two teacher-leaders) was so strong that it deployed itself differently as it best suited the group needs over time. At one point, for example, the three leaders decided that the assistant principal, Carolyn Gannon, would be silent during meetings as a strategy to bring a resistant teacher on board. In various ways across the building, the school was growing leaders. As Cohort 1 teacher-leaders became assistant principals (in and outside of New Dorp), new teacher-leaders were being groomed and emerged to take their places. As the work deepened, it seemed there were more and more opportunities for teacher leadership. And those who became the inquiry stars—the best at designing granular assessments, for example, or at leading their colleagues to do so—were often not the people anyone would have expected. One particularly quiet teacher, for example, who was not interested in formal administration at that point, surprised her colleagues and herself by becoming one of the most skilled facilitators of inquiry with resistant colleagues.

HOW THE SUBSTANCE OF INQUIRY EVOLVED

The early work of New Dorp's first cohort progressed through the stages shown in figure 5.4. In the first year, target students' identified skill gaps (bottom row) clustered in three areas, which then spurred schoolwide initiatives in vocabulary, writing, and math as a response. But the content of each initiative was relatively general in this first year, as were the learning targets that informed them. The vocabulary initiatives varied by department, for example, and results were not closely monitored. Use of a graphic organizer in English and social studies classes gave student writing a bit of a lift but not enough. System responses in math were more effective. Having clearly identified fractions as a high-leverage gap, the teams led improvement in all four subsystems: what was taught (basic skills), when (earlier and again closer to the test), by whom (stronger teachers who moved to the ninth grade), and how (with spiraled instruction).

Over the next five years, New Dorp's inquiry engine became more sophisticated and precise. As inquiry grew to involve first Cohort 2 and then all teachers, the principal, cabinet, and inquiry leaders began to see themselves as overseeing a large research operation. Teachers were learning the skills and habits needed for inquiry-based improvement and thus strategic inquiry was shifting school culture; but at the same time, inquiry leaders were paying close attention to what was being learned. Patterns were emerging. Once math teams closed foundational skill gaps (basic operations, signed numbers, etc.), students were getting stuck in word problems, especially multistep problems. In science, students struggled to express the relationship between ideas, even at the sentence level. In English and social studies, students struggled with writing skills as fundamental as distinguishing a specific from a general statement and using transitions such as *first, second, third.*

FIGURE 5.4   New Dorp High School Cohort 1: Focus of new SLC teams' strategic inquiry

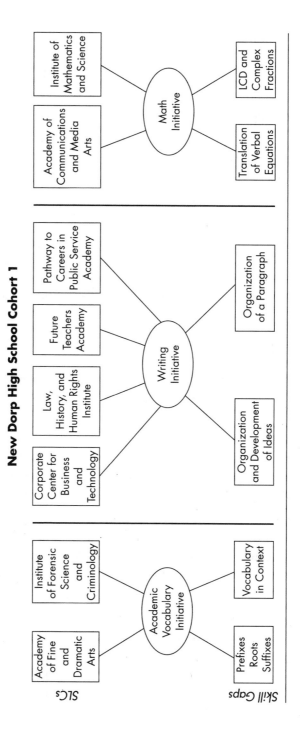

New Dorp High School Cohort 1

After two and a half years of schoolwide inquiry (three years since Cohort 1 began its work), New Dorp's internal inquiry leaders felt the need for change. They looked at the findings across the school's thirty-six-plus inquiry teams and saw the pattern: students struggled most with writing and/or with the foundational prerequisites for complex thinking and expression that writing strategies promote. Two years earlier Natasha had introduced strategies from an outside writing program called Teaching Basic Writing Skills since it seemed to target and develop exactly those areas that the inquiry teams were identifying as deficient. Principal DeAngelis saw the value of the program but felt strongly that the timing for introducing it to her school was not right. "First we have to cultivate the need," she said. Two years later that's what happened. Large numbers of teachers knew exactly where students were getting stuck. In the spring of 2010, DeAngelis and her cabinet felt it was time to aggregate the learning across teams and to develop a unified, systemic response.

The following September New Dorp launched its version of Teaching Basic Writing Skills across the ninth grade.[3] The work took off most in social studies, where Dina Zoleo, a Cohort 1 teacher-leader whose team had focused on writing, became the assistant principal and where the prior department chair had left a strong content-based curriculum and common assessments to build on. Zoleo and a core group of teachers worked with Judith Hochman, an expert consultant and the developer of Teaching Basic Writing Skills, to develop daily writing activities to support literacy concurrent with social studies content. Many teachers resisted, worried about sacrificing content. The rapid improvements in students' content knowledge and writing ability, however, quickly brought around the dissenters, and by end of the following year the entire department was on board.

To date, this work has spread to the math, English, science, and physical education departments, which now all draw on common writing strategies in support of content objectives and to build writing, reading, and thinking skills. This required a big time commitment and a steep learning curve. High school teachers do not see themselves primarily as writing teachers, and they are not generally confident and comfortable in teaching writing. When they saw the results, however, and were offered the needed professional development and support, the teachers came around and became energized—as did the students. During the first year of implementation, teachers started to hear the buzz about the new Common Core State Standards. They heard that soon students would be required to read and write in more sophisticated ways than were currently required and that there would be particular emphasis on argumentative and persuasive writing and on analyzing documents and presenting evidence persuasively for an informed, selected point of view. Those New Dorp teachers most deeply immersed in the new writing program embraced these standards, feeling that, for the first time, they had the tools that would enable all their students to meet them."Without these strategies," Zoleo said, "kids are going to hit those Common Core assessments and fall further and further behind. They're going to give up. With these strategies, we can get our kids there."

Members of Cohort 1—the principal, administrators, and teacher-leaders who had been shaping and facilitating New Dorp's evolution—say that without strategic inquiry, the school's teachers would not have recognized the value of the writing strategies; they would have thought the strategies were babyish. But in learning exactly what skills their students needed to acquire, they recognized its strategies as solutions.

SYSTEMATIZING INQUIRY

For the first five years, New Dorp's new SLCs used common planning time to solidify each SLC's culture, to learn strategic inquiry, and to identify skill gaps. Between 2006 and 2011, SLC teams used common planning time for inquiry. Having built strong SLCs, learned the strategic inquiry process, shifted school culture, and identified a high-priority area of struggle (writing), teachers and assistant principals now needed more time to strengthen their departments and to build curriculum that responded to the identified gaps. In 2011 DeAngelis programmed teachers' common time by departments. Teachers used their daily meeting time to align the curriculum with the new writing program and with CCSS. For the following school year (2012–2013), the faculty voted to allocate more time for teacher collaboration than was mandated in the teacher contract. Beginning in the fall of 2012, teachers continued to meet for daily common time by department and for an additional two-hour block weekly by SLCs.

Because its strategies target high-leverage skill gaps—areas where backfilling fundamentals develops content, writing, oral expression, and reading comprehension simultaneously—New Dorp's writing program serves as a unifying force for schoolwide instructional coherence. The principal's clear message is that consistent implementation of the writing strategies is the primary way the school will close the gap between where students are and the high performance bar set by CCSS and is the primary driver of improved teaching effectiveness. For example, strategies that develop students' written expression simultaneously improve formative assessment practices and "accountable talk."[4] Instructional improvement aligns the prioritized student skill gaps with consistent, skilled implementation of strategies that work to close them.

Recent visitors to New Dorp, when learning about its past and current structures for teacher collaboration, asked the principal, "If common time is being used for curriculum development, where is inquiry happening now?" DeAngelis paused for a moment to think and then said, "We don't really need a structure for inquiry anymore. It's everywhere now. It's just the way we think."

CREATING A SCHOOL INQUIRY CULTURE: LEADERSHIP PIPELINE AND FRESH-START STRATEGIES

Other schools tipped their cultures toward strategic inquiry using approaches that differed from New Dorp's. While sticking to the core principles, these schools' leaders and facilitators adapted to and took advantage of particular context conditions to chart their course toward changing the school culture. A couple of examples illustrate that one change strategy does not fit all. Nonetheless, school leaders and facilitators in each school had to grapple with the challenges of staging the change process, navigating resistance, and using strategic inquiry to move students and adults.

Creating a Pipeline of Certified Inquiry Leaders

Hillcrest, a large high school in Queens, developed an inquiry culture by developing a pipeline of teachers who participated in the Baruch College credentialing program that spawned strategic inquiry. It took the opportunity created by a multiyear grant supporting schools' participation in the program to build a critical mass of program graduates ready to lead strategic inquiry. This approach contrasts with New Dorp's, where the certification program played no role in the change process. With Hillcrest being one of four high schools that piloted the program, Principal Stephen Duch and other school leaders had a voice and sense of ownership in the program's evolution, so the pipeline strategy for school change made sense. Further, given its size and the number of participants it recruited (nine–twelve teachers for each of four program cohorts), the school was able to hold the weekly program seminars on campus and significantly streamline the logistical costs of teacher participation.

Hillcrest's pipeline strategy grew out of its pilot year in the Baruch certification program, when the participating teacher team identified the school's size and impersonal structure as a major source of student failure. The team's research revealed that struggling students were not aware of the services available to support them and recommended restructuring the school into SLCs that could provide more personalized support to students. Given compelling evidence and rationale, the school moved forward on structural reform, and Principal Duch saw the Baruch credentialing program as a key opportunity to develop inquiry leadership across the new SLCs. Twelve teachers selected for the next program cohort were assigned as directors or codirectors of the school's nine new SLCs. Subsequent cohorts of program participants/graduates built a solid pipeline of well-trained strategic inquiry leaders in each SLC.

This strategy for school culture change engendered initial resistance from assistant principals, whose positions and roles were rooted in the traditional subject department structure. Resistance came in part from restructuring and the SLC directors' new leadership roles and resource control. It also came also from a shift in the school's approach to improving student achievement through data-based inquiry to identify and address student learning needs. Strategic inquiry challenged the school's prior emphasis on improving instruction through administrative supervision and teacher professional development in content instruction. Some assistant principals resisted this shift in strategy and in their authority. But after the first year of struggle, Hillcrest had successfully redefined the assistant principal role as content specialists in support of inquiry-based reform. The principal described the new design as "similar to a district structure with the principal as superintendent, assistant principals as district office staff, and SLC directors/codirectors as principals."

Culture change came about gradually in this large restructured high school. Successive cohorts of Baruch-trained inquiry teams worked with their colleagues to diagnose student learning needs as the basis for instruction. The first program cohort tested ways of involving teachers of the target students in classroom observations (LITs), initially focusing on how to communicate about the work in ways that made them comfortable with the observations. Team members then experimented with ways of sharing their transcripts so that a teacher could learn to see the class through the lens of struggling students and make adjustments. They learned from experience in data sharing what resonated with their SLC colleagues. Later cohorts, prompted by Phase III of strategic inquiry, worked to bring about and sustain the culture shifts that were occurring within and across all the SLCs.

Hillcrest also developed its own strategic inquiry facilitator. Assistant Principal Dan Scanlon was coinstructor for the third cohort of teacher participants, developing facilitation skills by working alongside Felicia Hirata, a skilled external facilitator, and being part of the weekly facilitator meetings at Baruch. The model of an external-internal facilitator partnership was effective in accelerating teams' progress. Hirata was able to push in ways an internal facilitator cannot; however, Scanlon had immediate access and influence, and investing in his deep development had immediate and continued long-term payoff in student progress. According to the principal and other school leaders, as well as evidence from annual teacher surveys, the school reached a tipping point during the third year when a critical mass of teachers had completed the SAM credential-ing program and were leading their SLC colleagues in strategic inquiry. As more and more teachers became involved in the credentialing program, the work of successive cohorts accelerated. As Principal Duch put it, stra-tegic inquiry "is seen as an agent of change within the school. And the SAM participants have morphed into being the leaders of change." And regarding the third cohort of SAM teams in Hillcrest (twelve teachers in three teams), Duch was "amazed [by] the rapid pace at which they caught onto the work that we were doing in the class. That made me realize that we had really changed the culture of our building."

Fresh-Starting a School Inquiry Culture

Blackstone Elementary School in Boston used a very different strategy to create an inquiry culture. In this case, two educators who had part-nered with Baruch instructors to become skilled strategic inquiry facilita-tors seized the opportunity of restarting a turnaround elementary school. With most students outside the sphere of success, and 85 percent of the teachers new to the school, Principal Steve Zrike and Accelerated Im-provement director Lisa Lineweaver felt a sense of urgency and took on the challenge of creating a school culture in which strategic inquiry would be the norm from the start. In effect, they began with the model's third phase and with themselves as skilled inquiry facilitators and school leaders.

Lineweaver described the strategy: "[We] hypothesized that organiz-ing the school to make evidence-based inquiry practices routine at every level of the system would be a powerful route to speedily, systematically, and sustainably expand the school's sphere of success."[5] She and Zrike rea-soned that if they didn't immediately address the baseline conditions of learning, they would be enabling instructional chaos and allowing kids to fall further behind. They set out "to establish evidence-based inquiry as simply 'the way we work here,' with structures, practice, and culture es-tablished simultaneously across the school." Because they were seasoned strategic inquiry facilitators, they could move forward without the initial stage of training a cohort of teachers to move their colleagues. Building on their experience and Boston's history of whole-school improvement, they launched and led strategic inquiry with grade-level teacher teams across the preK–5 grade school.

As at New Dorp and Hillcrest, Blackstone's leaders used their positional authority to manage real and potential resistance to change. In this case, school administrators established conditions and ground rules needed for inquiry to develop and thrive. These included organizational structures; learning time at team and school levels; meeting structures, norms, tasks; decision rules for instruction and interventions; data systems; and expectations for data use. They charged all seven grade-level teams with using their common planning and professional development time to track their students' progress toward grade-level proficiency and to design interventions to get all students on track.

Based on their earlier experience as strategic inquiry facilitators, and particularly given the school's turnaround status and the fact that in some grades fully 70 percent of students were performing below standards, Blackstone's leaders anticipated teacher resistance to being asked to go small by starting with a target group of students when they could accurately say that their entire class deserved to be in the target group. They curtailed this source of resistance strategically, realizing that when faced with pervasive underperformance and so many teachers new to the school, their first leverage points must be to tend to the baseline conditions of learning: clear expectations about who was teaching what, to whom, how often, and to what level of mastery. Thus, they made a distinction between starting narrow and starting small. Instead of focusing on a set of target students outside the sphere of success as the driver for inquiry, and then drilling down into student work and data to identify specific skill gaps, Blackstone embraced a response to intervention (RTI) framework as a way to be explicit about teachers' need to examine and address the daily "literacy diet" in instruction for *all* students and to *then* go small to diagnose learning needs that require additional intervention. The RTI approach, required by federal special education policy, guides teachers in identifying and responding to individual student needs in a pyramid of interventions. In RTI, Tier 1 involves strong, systematic instruction and differentiation taking place during normal instruction for all students; Tier 2 interventions are more intense, occurring in small groups on top of (not instead of) Tier 1 instruction; Tier 3 interventions are individualized, typically carried out by certified special education teachers through a formal individual education plan (IEP). The RTI model calls for teachers to use frequent curriculum-based assessments to match students to appropriate instruction and interventions and thus can be a vehicle for building inquiry into teachers' work across the school.

In keeping with the strategic inquiry principle of changing school culture by building on what matters to teachers—the requirement that they use an RTI framework to diagnose and address student needs—embedding inquiry in RTI strategy made sense. Strategic inquiry directly addressed the challenges that elementary teachers face in learning to assess and respond flexibly to individual learning needs. As Lineweaver explained, "The RTI framework is helping us 'organize' our inquiry into multiple simultaneous cycles, with distinct learning targets and manageable action-steps for Tier 1 instruction and Tier 2 and 3 interventions; but it does not lessen the challenge of being a turnaround school trying to improve all areas at once."

Dedicated to developing teachers' strategic inquiry reflex, Blackstone's leaders have been continuously monitoring each of the seven grade-level teams' inquiry work and facilitating their moves toward deeper practice. During the three years since restarting the school, Lineweaver and current principal Cynthia Paris Jeffries have used system levers to build teachers' skills in strategic inquiry. By creating lower-grade and upper-grade data teams that learn to facilitate inquiry with their grade-level teams and use inquiry to move systems (e.g., targeted changes in curriculum, pacing, and interventions), they have spread and deepened inquiry leadership across the school. Most recent standardized test results attest to their progress on inquiry-based improvement: Blackstone met all thirteen performance targets in 2012 and far exceeded nine of them. The school stands out as an example of how strategic inquiry can be leveraged and facilitated from the top, as well as demonstrating the potential for accelerating culture change by marrying strategic inquiry and RTI at the elementary grade school level.

FALLING SHORT: SPECIALIST, HUB, AND DELEGATION PATTERNS

Yet, many schools that took up strategic inquiry in New York City and elsewhere fell short of creating a schoolwide inquiry culture. They didn't seriously take on the third phase of the model. Because New York City required schools to create inquiry teams, evaluators had the opportunity to study implementation in some of the schools that fell short.

Schools that did not invest in developing broad leadership for inquiry-based improvement tended toward three patterns (see figure 5.5). In one, the *specialist* pattern, a staff member or administrator takes responsibility for data-based inquiry and for deciding on interventions that may or may not involve classroom teachers. In the *hub* pattern a school team composed of administrators and teachers who represent different units carries out the inquiry process and determines instructional interventions and system changes without involving other teachers in the inquiry. In the third, *delegation* pattern all teachers are assigned to an inquiry team, but the school invests little in the training or support of team leaders who then are unprepared to facilitate strategic inquiry practice and culture shifts.

FIGURE 5.5   Implementation patterns that fall short of developing a school inquiry culture

Pattern	Description
Specialist	Locates responsibility for inquiry with the data specialist, who manages student performance data, uses inquiry to identify and diagnose needs of struggling students, and works with students to set goals and determine interventions; teachers are more or less brought into supporting interventions with individual students.
Hub	Locates collaborative inquiry primarily in a school team composed of administrator(s) and several teachers from different content areas; other teachers are more or less involved in carrying out interventions with target students.
Delegation	Characterized by breadth with limited depth of inquiry, in which all teachers meet regularly in grade-level teams and examine student performance data to identify gaps and decide on interventions for struggling students but lack leadership to develop rigor and mutual accountability for results.

Schools that failed to develop an inquiry culture after four years into New York City's inquiry initiative were alike in one important respect: the school administration did not make strategic inquiry *the* engine for school improvement or invest in developing a critical mass of change leaders. They complied with the letters but not the spirit or intent of the city's department of education policy.

Specialist Pattern

A small 7–12 grade school we'll call Frontier Academy, which had a relatively strong track record for its high-poverty student population, delegated responsibility for strategic inquiry to Assistant Principal Donovan. Following education department policy, Donovan became the school's data specialist and an active participant in the cross-school data specialist network designed to support data use and collaborative inquiry in the schools. Although the whole administrative team reviewed data on student performance patterns, it was Donovan's responsibility to carry out the detailed analyses of individual student data to identify and address particular skill gaps.

Frontier Academy's decision to compartmentalize inquiry in this way avoided disrupting school routines, which included providing individualized supports to students through an advisory program involving all teachers. The principal chose to buffer the teachers from extra demands of learning fine-grained data analysis to detect and address particular skill gaps and moving from individual accountability for particular student support to shared accountability for all students. The system was working well in motivating students to meet high academic standards and producing high rates of graduation and college attendance.

The downside of protecting teaching norms and routines was the missed opportunity to strengthen the school's academic support systems. Donovan struggled to meet the needs of students who evidenced particular skill gaps, making appointments with those students during cracks of the day or after school to share data with them and make a plan to address the gap. The better and more fine-grained the data became, the better he was able to identify students' needs, and the more overwhelming the job became. Struggling students came to see Donovan as a key academic resource, and his office became a whirlwind of student comings and goings.

In this pattern, a school data specialist or administrator effectively takes on the work that the strategic inquiry model envisions being carried out by teams of teachers across the school. An individual in this role is likely to be overwhelmed by demands of responding to evidence of student learning needs and is constrained in his ability to make system changes. This pattern does not appear to be sustainable beyond a few years.

Hub Pattern

A small themed high school we'll call Outreach Academy embraced strategic inquiry and sent successive teacher teams to the SAM credentialing program. The first SAM cohort formed a school inquiry team that continued for three years, adding new cohorts of two to three teachers each year. The school inquiry team has grown to include nearly a fourth of the faculty, and its inquiry practice is well-grounded in the strategic inquiry model. The team periodically reports inquiry data to the whole faculty, showing particular skill gaps for target students, describing interventions (and occasionally calling on teachers of target students to get involved), and providing evidence of results.

In the first three years of the school's strategic inquiry work, annual teacher survey data showed growth in reports of teachers using multiple kinds of student assessment data and school leaders using data for decision making. Yet the school did not reach a critical mass of teachers involved in strategic inquiry or a significant culture shift. Evidence-based practice and shared accountability for improving student achievement still resides largely in the school inquiry team.

Here, too, school leaders avoided disrupting established routines that define the school's mission and an intensive work life for its teachers. They counted on the incentive for teachers to get an administrative credential through the SAM program to gradually build the school's capacity for using the model to improve target students' achievement. The program participants report struggling to keep up with the assignments and feeling inhibited from calling on their colleagues to support specific interventions, respecting their heavy work demands. Each team felt pressed to limit its inquiry work to students in their own classes to avoid burdening other teachers. These teacher-leaders see their potential to lead inquiry in the school, beyond the school team, to be constrained by the intensity of teaching demands in the school. Nonetheless, the team has designed system changes that better serve student needs. For example, a recent SAM team prompted a new step in the school's portfolio assessment system so that it now provides timely formative feedback to students.

Outreach Academy and its pattern of inquiry implementation illustrate the special challenge of developing an inquiry culture on top of a highly institutionalized, demanding instructional program. In all schools, strategic inquiry leaders face the challenges of creating new time in the schedule for team meetings and engaging teachers in new work beyond classroom teaching. In the small themed high schools that New York City has spawned, teachers' work already entails collaboration with colleagues to implement the instructional program, and in Outreach this work includes assessing student portfolios and accompanying students in educational travel. There is little slack in their time or attention to take on the significant strategic inquiry learning process schoolwide. In general, over the years of the SAM certification program, teacher teams from small themed high schools struggled most to get traction for inquiry-based reform in their schools.[6]

In this particular context, the hub pattern makes sense as a way to institutionalize inquiry-based decision making at the top of the organization and create a cadre of trained leaders with broad reach across the school. There is no question that the growing school team has made a big difference in the success of its target students, and it is positioned to make system changes in response to its inquiry. The fact that the faculty respects and goes along with the school team's evidence-based decision making is a small but significant culture shift.

Delegation Pattern

Another small themed high school, which we'll call Growth Academy, sent one four-person team to the SAM program and positioned team members to lead inquiry in each of four cross-discipline grade-level teams. Although the principal authorized the SAM graduates' leadership and planned to recommend one of them to replace her as principal when she retired, these new inquiry team leaders lacked sufficient experience and support for re-culturing the school.

The SAM program did not sufficiently prepare these teachers to navigate the challenges of leading change with a group of a dozen colleagues. For example, a graduate charged with leading the ninth grade team was stumped when a colleague commented, in response to his sharing fine-grained data on individual student performance on an English language arts assessment, that a particular student who performed poorly is just "lazy." This inquiry team leader hadn't yet mastered the facilitation moves it takes to focus the conversation on particular skill gaps and to enforce using evidence to diagnose and address a student's academic needs. In effect, a teaching culture that blames students for failure and gives teachers little hope that they can make a difference was not changed.

The fate of strategic inquiry at Growth Academy points to the need for a well-trained internal or external facilitator to deepen and sustain teachers' change leadership with colleagues. And it suggests that a school needs to involve a critical mass of teachers in strategic inquiry training—enough that each school inquiry team is led by at least a pair of trained teachers. These teacher facilitators can then collaborate and support one another in keeping their colleagues on track with strategic inquiry and shifting their beliefs and, ultimately, the school culture.

Strategic inquiry is designed to tip a school culture toward shared accountability, evidence-based practice, and distributed leadership within a few years. Achieving a self-sustaining culture shift depends on school administrators' sticking with this approach and making sure that successive teacher teams get trained in using and facilitating it. Also key is having or bringing in a facilitator who is deeply steeped in strategic inquiry to train the first team(s) so that they learn to implement all phases effectively and can facilitate inquiry with colleagues.

In Phase III, team members step into the role of leading their colleagues to experience the same shifts in practice and beliefs that they experienced in earlier phases. In doing so, they carry the moral authority of the work—enforcing norms against labeling students to account for their academic skill gaps, for example—and think and act strategically about how to lead organizational change and develop shared accountability for results. Schools in which growing numbers of teachers have taken on these leadership roles have achieved stunning results.

PART III

SYSTEM SUPPORT OF INQUIRY-BASED REFORM

Realizing the vision of continuous school improvement through evidence-based decision making takes more than individual schools deciding to use strategic inquiry as a tested model for change and capacity building. It takes professional capacities and inquiry resources developed beyond school walls. Especially important are school districts and teacher and administrator credentialing programs.

Districts make a big difference for schools' progress on this reform vision because, for one, a school is much more likely to take up this reform strategy when its district administrators make it a system priority. In most school systems across the country, the central office is the place where decisions about improvement strategies are made and resources to support them are allocated. Also, a district can be more or less successful in supporting and sustaining its schools' progress on strategic inquiry. The kinds of system capacities that matter most are well-trained facilitators and administrators who can lead change in professional culture at all levels of the system.

Local administrator credentialing programs play a role in nurturing or inhibiting this reform direction as well. Graduates of a program aligned with strategic inquiry, like the SAM program in New York City, are ready to step into administrator positions and lead the change process. In fact, they lead inquiry to improve student achievement in their schools while participating in the program. A pipeline of credentialed leaders of strategic inquiry is a key resource for districts that otherwise, after filling positions with graduates of traditional programs, face the challenge of training their site administrators to lead inquiry-driven school change.

For better or worse, district central offices and local administrator preparation programs matter for how well a school progresses on inquiry-based improvement. But how and in what ways can each build capacity for school change to a strategic inquiry culture? In addressing this question for districts, we draw on evidence from New York City's Children First Initiative, launched in 2003–2004 to improve student achievement through greater school autonomy and accountability, and from other districts with sustained investments in collaborative inquiry as their primary approach to instructional improvement and point to challenges district leaders have faced in staying the course.[1] For administrator preparation programs, we describe how the SAM program evolved over time and developed its capacity to both develop inquiry leaders and improve student achievement in the participants' schools.

CHAPTER 6

Developing a District System of Inquiry-Based Improvement

Districts cannot mandate culture shifts. But they can create conditions that make a big difference for whether or not their schools become places where teachers share accountability for student success, use evidence to make decisions about instruction, and step up to lead improvement. District administrators can lead change toward this vision in ways that honor and build on principals' and teachers' commitments and professionalism, instead of triggering a compliance mentality through bureaucratic management approaches. As crucial is making strategic inquiry the primary engine for improving student success across schools over the long haul and not wavering from this capacity-building district reform strategy.

WHY STRATEGIC INQUIRY AS THE PRIMARY DISTRICT REFORM STRATEGY?

The most compelling reason for pursuing strategic inquiry is its track record for achieving steady improvement in student achievement over time. While some programs or reform approaches can bring about a temporary boost or jump in student achievement, strategic inquiry is distinct in that it develops educators' ability to continuously diagnose and address student learning needs and needed changes in school systems. It is not "implemented" once and for all; rather, it is a model for developing a school's capacity to keep improving student success.

Despite a strong rationale for making strategic inquiry a top priority for district improvement, this reform approach may not appeal to district administrators and school boards because it is neither a quick fix nor new and sexy. Those looking for a simple answer to the question "What works?" might be disappointed to learn that developing school and district capacity for evidence-based decision making takes several years. District decision makers will need to make a commitment to building professionals' capacity to use evidence to make steady improvement over the long haul. Also, because the idea of inquiry-based reform has been around for awhile, some veteran administrators and teachers may have given up on this approach. As one urban district superintendent commented after hearing about the strategic inquiry model, "Didn't we do the 'cycle of inquiry' ten or twenty years ago [under a different initiative], and didn't we find out that it doesn't work?" Our response was, "Well, you can decide that it's a bad idea to develop schools' capacity to use evidence as a way to improve student achievement, or you can decide that it's a good idea but implementation fell short." He responded, "Aha! It's the second, and I hadn't thought about it that way."

Although researchers have studied the implementation problems associated with prior inquiry initiatives, district leaders haven't benefited from the lessons learned—for example, that providing a big picture for inquiry doesn't bring about shifts in teachers' ideas about why students fail or whether they can make a difference and that relying on external facilitators doesn't grow inquiry leadership in schools and districts. Strategic inquiry as a model for educational improvement addresses the specific limitations of earlier inquiry initiatives, especially in specifying a clear design that starts small and systematically develops teacher leadership. Still, its successful implementation depends on district and school leaders' making it a priority and investing sufficient resources and strategic leadership to leverage and support change.

Once district leaders commit to strategic inquiry as a system reform priority, they face the implementation challenge. What does it take for a district to develop school leaders' and teachers' capacity for progress and sustained commitment to continuous inquiry-based improvement? The answer hinges on three things: establishing system conditions and resources, leading culture change, and staying the course.

ESTABLISHING CONDITIONS FOR STRATEGIC INQUIRY

First and foremost as a condition for progress, administrators need to communicate clearly and frequently to teachers and other stakeholders that collaborative inquiry is the district's primary school reform approach and then act in accordance with the message. This means that other district and school approaches to improving instruction, including teacher professional development in best practices of content instruction, will take a back seat until strategic inquiry is embedded in school routines.

This doesn't mean a school cannot take on other initiatives, but doing so requires careful thought about how staff time and attention is allocated and how any additional initiative fits with strategic inquiry. Especially in the first year or two, administrators and teachers will be focused on learning strategic inquiry principles and practices; pulling them in another direction would compete for their time and attention. Initiatives that mesh with strategic inquiry are those that support teacher teams in addressing the needs of particular students, such as instruction for English language learners, or that define clear student learning standards and assessments, such as the new CCSS. Once teacher teams are skilled in using strategic inquiry, they are ready to take on a new district initiative aimed at improving their diagnosis of and response to student learning needs.

In establishing strategic inquiry as a district priority, principals need to be brought on board with the reform agenda and to become familiar with its principles and phases in order to help leverage school teams' progress, as well as protect teachers from other demands on their learning and time out of the classroom. Teachers need an introduction to strategic inquiry that gives them evidence that it can produce better results for their students than other approaches and that sets clear expectations of what it entails on their part and how they will be supported. Accountability relationships need to shift from top down to shared responsibility at the school level. District offices must authorize schools' data-based decision making and hold them accountable for results while providing support for their progress in using data to improve student achievement.

Making It a Priority

To communicate the priority for inquiry-based reform district administrators are challenged to convey the rationale in ways that are meaningful and convincing to principals and teachers. Some districts take advantage of the DuFour PLC workshops.[1] These one- or two-day sessions bring together principals and teacher teams from a large district or from multiple small districts and convince them that student achievement improves when teacher teams use data to address their students' learning needs on a regular basis. They use research-based evidence to convey a moral imperative for teachers to work together, regularly assess student learning to standards, and design interventions to ensure student mastery, suggesting that to not do so is akin to malpractice in medicine. These sessions can set the stage and develop teachers' and principals' appetites for inquiry as a primary improvement strategy. Although the sessions put forth a general PLC design, the main takeaway is commitment to the vision.

To move schools toward internal accountability (versus meeting district or state requirements), district administrators need to create system accountability mechanisms that match this intent. New York City, for example, launched its collaborative inquiry initiative as a way to build schools' capacity to succeed in the district's broader Children First reform. The city's education department signaled, and then put teeth into, this approach to school improvement with two new accountability mechanisms: the Quality Review, designed initially to track a school's progress on teachers' collaborative inquiry; and the Progress Report, a way of grading schools that gives credit for progress, especially with struggling students, rather than just overall performance.[2]

Making strategic inquiry *the* approach to developing school capacity for inquiry-based improvement requires more than central office policy and broader commitment to the general reform approach. It requires that district staff and external support providers share an understanding of how the model works and its core principles. Even when the district intent is to prioritize strategic inquiry, as was the case in New York City during early years of Children First, central office staffs' understandings of what this means are not always consistent. Not all district staff pushed messages in the intended way. For example, some deemphasized the importance of using granular formative assessment data systematically, and only some of the decentralized networks of schools invested time and resources in intensive workshops that brought teacher-leaders and principals together to develop their understandings of strategic inquiry principles and build practical knowledge about how to implement them. In these networks, school administrators communicated and led the inquiry work in ways that avoided a compliance response found elsewhere and engaged teachers in serious effort to use the inquiry model to improve their students' success.

Creating Time

A districtwide schedule that includes common time for teachers to meet regularly is a key condition for collaborative inquiry. The district calendar might specify weekly or biweekly late-start days or early-release days, in which teachers' instructional time is devoted to team meetings to diagnose and design responses to assessed student learning needs. This entails negotiating time within the union contract or renegotiating the contract, as well as convincing parents that teachers' time working together will benefit their students more than the lost classroom time. Once teacher meeting times are officially scheduled, their effective use for collaborative inquiry depends on site administrators' protecting the time, enforcing teacher participation, and providing facilitator training and support. In the NYC schools that created common planning time on a daily basis, such as New Dorp High School, strategic inquiry had the biggest benefits for students.

Forging Alignment in the Central Office

This reform agenda calls for changing central office practices to align with a school-based, bottom-up approach to instructional improvement. Strategic inquiry puts teacher teams in the driver's seat of reform, where they are making evidence-based judgments about instruction that traditionally are made by specialists in a district central office. Rather than directing schools to implement particular programs or practices, central office administrators and staff face the challenge of responding to schools' particular, evidence-based needs for support. As with strategic inquiry used to address student learning needs, district staff use evidence of specific school improvement needs, identified through inquiry carried out by the school and/or by the central office, to develop a response. For example, a district may use a developmental rubric to rate each school's strategic inquiry capacity in order to determine the kind and level of facilitator support needed. Or schools may have identified a particular student learning gap that warrants district resource allocation. Key is the use of evidence to determine how the central office and particular departments act to support school improvement. District administrators and specialists can enhance teacher teams' capacity to accelerate student learning in two ways: by customizing and coordinating their support of inquiry practice in schools at different stages of development and by supporting responses to specific student learning needs identified through inquiry.

Perhaps hardest for district administrators is mobilizing staff and resources of central office departments—the silos created by federal and state funding lines, specialized services, and grants—in support of inquiry-based school improvement. This entails breaking down silos to create coherent and coordinated support to address particular school needs. For example, district subject departments that provide or broker teacher training in content instruction (English, mathematics, science, history, languages, etc.) are typically disconnected from the special education department that oversees policy for identifying special needs students and developing individual interventions (IEPs) and monitoring their progress. In such districts, schools like Blackstone Elementary face an uphill struggle when they try to forge a coherent approach to meeting student needs through a continuum of regular and special education instruction. Coherent school support from these two district departments requires that they *together* look at data to identify patterns of student learning needs in each school and work out a plan for coordinating their support and that they are ready to respond jointly to school requests for help in addressing particular student needs. This is happening in Sanger Unified in California, which has made steady gains in student achievement across all seventeen district schools since it adopted an inquiry-based reform strategy in 2005. These departments work together in helping teachers at all district schools to address special student needs in the classroom and to identify when students need special education services.[3]

Beyond creating central office department collaboration to support schools' identified needs, a district needs to establish routines for data-based decision making between the district and school. This both enforces the norm of evidence-based practice in the district and defines the focus of their shared accountability for improving student performance. Occasions for data-based dialogue between each school and district administrators and staff need to be built into the district calendar. Protocols for annual or regular convenings set the stage: specifying *when* particular positions/people come together to examine *which* specific kinds of data in order to make *what* collective data-based decisions. Such dialogue generates focus and shared accountability for school improvement and impetus for collaboration among district departments.

In districts advanced in inquiry-based improvement, like California's Long Beach Unified and Sanger Unified, there is an institutionalized structure for data-based decision making between the central office and the schools.[4] Sanger, for example, has annual fall Principal Summit where each principal presents an analysis of student performance on the previous year's California State Test and points to priorities for improvement that set the course for district support for the year, with ongoing follow-up and tweaking. In Long Beach, district leaders hold monthly day-long Key Results meetings with principals, a practice launched more than a decade ago with the district's middle school reform effort. Although practices have evolved somewhat differently for schools at each grade level, the meetings include a review of multiple measures on district benchmark assessments and observations that surface challenges for the school or particular groups within the school. At the high school level, administrators and teachers from across the district conduct Key Results Walk-Throughs at each school three times a year. The qualitative observation data and specific feedback from the visiting team help schools draw connections between their assessment data and instructional practices, as well as establish ongoing data-based conversations between district and school leaders. One Long Beach high school principal explained:

> The [Key Results Walk-Throughs] are really eye openers that give your school, [through] the eyes of representatives from the other high schools and from the central office, a chance to listen to and review your data with you and then walk through the classrooms and see if there's been any improvement on what the focus has been. I think that also helps them when we are looking at our different categories of students and where the gap is and how it's being closed. [It] is critical to what we do to.[5]

Note that these district routines mirror Phase II of strategic inquiry, in which school teams identify system conditions that inhibit student success. Here, at the district level, central office administrators help diagnose school needs that call for resources beyond school walls.

Both of these advanced inquiry districts developed a culture of data-based inquiry within the central office as well. In each, the district administrative team meets at least weekly to review data and problem-solve together and keeps the conversation going informally on a daily basis. They use evidence to make policy decisions, as when Long Beach abandoned Sylvan tutoring and Read 180 interventions because the data showed no improvement in student achievement. With leadership from district administrators and central office administrators and staff, the district's schools came to take inquiry-based decision making for granted.

BROKERING AND DEVELOPING RESOURCES

In addition to establishing priority and central office conditions for strategic inquiry, district administrations can broker or develop specific resources that help schools move forward: skilled facilitators, data systems that support formative assessments, and mechanisms for sharing evidence from inquiry across schools.

Training Facilitators

By far the most crucial resource for school progress on strategic inquiry is well-trained facilitators. This is because the model pushes against beliefs and norms common in the teaching profession—such as that students struggle because of their difficult personal lives or personalities and teachers can make little difference—and a skilled facilitator keeps a team on track in order to bring about shifts in beliefs that constrain progress. As shown in chapter 3, a skilled facilitator is especially important during Phase I of strategic inquiry when a team is most likely to get off course.

A district can develop facilitators skilled in strategic inquiry through a trainer-of-trainers approach. Initial trainers would need to be instructors or graduates of a strategic inquiry certification program or teachers who have been through all three inquiry phases with a skilled facilitator. An outside trainer could develop an initial cadre of district facilitators/trainers who might be drawn from existing coaches and teachers on special assignment and/or from teachers within a school or group of schools. These individuals would then become trainers of a broadening cadre of facilitators to support the strategic inquiry work of teacher teams in each district school.

To ensure sufficient quality and depth, the training needs to be carried out in one or more schools so that the inquiry is authentically focused on moving particular students, systems, and teachers. Developing a pipeline and critical mass of district trainers takes two or three years, depending on district size, but the capacity-building investment improves schools along the way. Because strategic inquiry marries school improvement with leadership development, the start-up costs are never without benefits in student achievement gains.

Realistically, the developmental time frame to train district leadership and a critical mass of facilitators and then achieve a tipping point toward an inquiry culture across district schools is roughly five years.[6] In New

York City, a growing cadre of strategic inquiry program graduates has moved into formal and informal facilitator roles over a period of four to five years. Some have become school administrators, others have become inquiry facilitators in one or another of the city's school networks, and still others are facilitating inquiry in teacher teams or SLCs in a school. In Sanger, the district trained lead teachers of elementary grade-level teams or secondary course teams through PLC workshops and regular, ongoing meetings in which the lead teachers share experiences to strengthen their facilitation skills. Some of them have moved into positions of department chair in a secondary school or school or district instructional support roles, extending their reach as inquiry facilitators.

Although the time entailed in developing a broad cadre of skilled facilitators may seem long, the strategic inquiry reform agenda aims to change the professional cultures of all schools. There is no shortcut to building a strong "middle system" of teacher leaders prepared to bring about school change to meet the needs of students who have persistently failed.

Enhancing Data Systems

A district can support team inquiry by enhancing its data system to include a wide variety of measures of student skills relevant to grade-level content standards. This is so that teachers can get an accurate picture of student performance gaps, as revealed by several assessments. Long Beach, for example, has a data system that includes several state tests and multiple district assessments and benchmarks; the benchmarks include results on curriculum-based assessments that teachers give every six to eight weeks and submit to the district. When correlated with state standards tests, the data help teachers target the specific skills that need addressing through instruction. Although many districts currently conduct semiannual or quarterly periodic assessments linked to state standards, which provide schools with benchmarks for tracking student progress toward proficiency, the data are neither granular nor frequent enough to support strategic inquiry.

Increasingly, software is available that makes it easy for teachers to enter and access formative assessment data on a regular basis and much more closely monitor student learning. In order to support teacher teams' assessments of student skill gaps and responses, however, the software must allow them to disaggregate assessment data by student and item within and across classrooms. For example, Sanger Unified adopted a data system technology that allows teachers to scan bubble test data with a wand and obtain immediate results. The system allows a teacher team to examine results for classes by student and test item and readily identify learning targets for struggling students. Such technology can support strategic inquiry in teacher teams and also help generate an appetite for data use among teachers new to inquiry.

Teacher teams new to strategic inquiry, or encountering new student learning standards, face the challenge of creating their own formative assessments within or across content areas. The district central office can support this assessment development work by providing as-needed professional development, on-site mentoring, and examples for teachers to model. As states and districts move toward the national Common Core State Standards and assessments, teacher teams will need expert help in creating or adapting formative assessments geared to the higher-order skills students are expected to master, such as justifying answers and making a claim with evidence. Ongoing formative assessment will need to be sufficiently granular to inform next teaching steps targeted to students' specific learning needs. Capacity building starts in the district office with hiring or preparing staff that deeply understand strategic inquiry and can work with teacher teams across schools in using new assessments to diagnose student skill gaps relevant to the new CCSS and help them bridge wide gaps. It is essential that these central office staff are either graduates of a certification program aligned with strategic inquiry or that they are led through a similar process prior to or while supporting the work in schools. It is highly unlikely, otherwise, that they can lead or support the work effectively.

Capturing Evidence from Strategic Inquiry

The SAM credentialing program has developed a wide range of strategic inquiry resources that districts, schools, and teachers might draw on. They support each inquiry phase and are meant to be used and adapted in local contexts. (See the appendixes for a sampling of these tools).[7]

A district-designed toolkit to support school teams' strategic inquiry might include information on inquiry results with the aim of accelerating teachers' capacity to identify and address student learning needs. For example, it could distill information and evidence about (1) key student learning gaps prevalent at each grade level and content area, such as weak graphing skills among ninth graders; (2) instructional interventions that show evidence of closing a particular gap, such as targeted instruction in teaching the concept of slope in algebra classes; and (3) examples of dramatic success of a particular program that combines strategies effective in addressing a key gap, such as the Teaching Basic Writing Skills program (see chapter 5). However, developing a valid, reliable, and useful district toolkit requires a strategy for collecting, aggregating, and making sense of information coming from schools and teacher teams and then deciding how to respond. Early in its Children's First initiative, New York City created a portal for teacher teams to post their work; but this was not enough to make the information useful. In order for a teacher team to be convinced that a particular instructional response to a specific skill gap resulted in a significant move in student achievement, they needed to see readily interpretable evidence; and in order to make good use of the information, they needed to be in a school where inquiry and evidence grounded instructional decisions.

The central office can play the useful role of collecting and distilling information and evidence to support the spread of good inquiry-based practice and to implement smart district-level systemic responses that accelerate student learning across schools. In this way, inquiry-based learning is truly nested, and the district becomes a learning organization at all levels. But this requires investments of time, structures, and leadership at the central office.

Figure 6.1 captures these bottom-line district conditions and resources for strategic inquiry, as well as the necessary shifts away from what is typical. But the challenge for leading change across district schools—including establishing these conditions and resources—goes beyond policy decisions and the nuts and bolts of strategic inquiry.

FIGURE 6.1   Establishing district conditions and resources for strategic inquiry

District outcomes	From . . .	To . . .
Policy and central office conditions		
Reform focus and priority for evidence-based decision making	Patchwork of programs and reform initiatives	Priority for strategic inquiry
District schedule that establishes and protects regular time for teachers' collaborative inquiry	Principal prerogative to schedule and run staff meetings	Principal responsible to protect teachers' common time for collaborative inquiry
Coordinated central office support for strategic inquiry	Department silos that bring specialized regulations and services to schools	Specialized services coordinated to provide coherent support to meet schools' identified needs
Resources for strategic inquiry		
Facilitators trained to support school teams' progress on strategic inquiry	Content coaches or teachers on special assignment who provide instructional support	Strategic inquiry facilitators trained to guide school teams in all inquiry phases (growing cadre)
Data systems to support teacher teams' formative assessments	Data systems for organizing and disseminating standardized test data	Data management system that allows school teams to enter and share results of formative assessments
Tools designed to support strategic inquiry	Curriculum programs and guides, standardized tests, and item banks	Strategic inquiry guidelines for school teams; formative assessments of specific skills; Web portals for sharing inquiry results and successful responses to specific skill gaps

LEADING CHANGE

Once district administrators decide to use strategic inquiry as the primary approach to improving student achievement, they face choices about how to implement it to bring about intended shifts in teachers' beliefs and school culture. Conditions that enable strategic inquiry—common time, coordinated services, data systems and tools—are not sufficient to engender change in teachers' work culture. As described in earlier chapters, principals and facilitators lead change within a school, but change across many schools depends on system leadership. Unfortunately, districts often make decisions about how to leverage change that actually work against it.

Our research points to two patterns that districts follow in directing change from the top that have very different consequences: *bureaucratic approaches* and *professional approaches*.[8] They reflect radically different conceptions of what it takes to achieve inquiry-based school improvement. Using a bureaucratic approach, district offices create rules, checklists, and sanctions to leverage implementation, but they backfire because they ignite teachers' resistance or prompt ritual compliance. For example, when one urban school district launched a PLC initiative, the central office hired a management consulting firm to help move the agenda forward in the newly restructured high schools. Bringing a management frame to the problem, the consultants created timelines and checklists for monitoring each school's implementation of teacher collaboration. But the benchmarks and timelines were out of touch with the practice and culture shifts needed for real implementation, so schools subject to sanctions under this regimen fell back to complying with the superficial criteria of time allocations for team meetings, teacher attendance rates, and the like. Evidence suggests that such bureaucratic tools and controls are not well-suited to leveraging and supporting schools' success in implementing strategic inquiry, particularly in an era when federal and state accountability systems have engendered a compliance mentality among many educators.

Using a professional approach to leading change in school culture, district leaders push against educators' common view that the central office, or "Downtown," constrains their judgment and erects bureaucratic hurdles that get in the way of their work. District leaders devote their time and communications to developing collaborative professional relationships focused on student learning. For example, in the district mentioned above, one central office administrator formed and led a PLC of all high school principals, creating a space for them in which to build shared understandings of the district vision for teacher PLCs, discuss their role in leading change, and get resources and advice on addressing issues at their sites. Some of the principals, in turn, created a PLC of assistant principals within their school who then learned together how better to support teacher teams working to improve student learning.

This example shows that the two approaches to implementing policy can coexist and compete within the same district central office. The bureaucratic approach pushed principals and teachers toward compliance, while the professional approach built school administrators' buy-in and capacity to lead change in their school and gave them the experience of using collaborative inquiry to improve their own practice in leading change.

Districts in which administrators and staff fully embrace a professional approach to leading change stand out against typical central office practice. They act on the same principles they promote for teachers—collaboration and evidence-based decision-making—within the central office and in their interactions with the schools. Most important, they build trusting, collaborative relationships between levels of the system. As a Long Beach district administrator put it,

> It's critical to establish trust and build the day-to-day relationships necessary to get the work done. Relationships are fragile. They are hardest to build, and the first to go. In our annual reviews, I talk with principals about the importance of their relationships with their staff and community and also with each other. People don't trust easily, so I am careful to establish a culture where trustworthiness, as well as instructionally competent principals, can flourish.[9]

In "professionalized" districts like Long Beach and Sanger, where schools made steady progress on student achievement for more than five consecutive years, administrators use structures and routines for collaborative inquiry between the central office and each district school that engender trust. As described earlier, both districts have a goal-setting process with schools at the beginning of the year that is revisited throughout the year. The Sanger Principal Summits and Long Beach Key Results meetings are strategic in engendering open communication and shared accountability between levels and setting the expectation that both parties will be using evidence to evaluate their success. They forge team spirit among the school and the central office personnel.

But developing effective district improvement practices of this sort requires that district leaders carefully balance top-down pressure for school improvement with support. They must go hand in hand. The bottom line is consistently communicating that improving student learning is a joint responsibility of the school and the central office, while making clear their expectations for ongoing school improvement. For instance, when Sanger administrators launched the Principal Summits in the early years of their inquiry-based reform, the principals were highly anxious. They lacked skills in analyzing data and worried about what might happen if they revealed their school's weakest areas. Within a year or two, the district culture had tipped to relationships of mutual respect and trust and a shared commitment to learning. Through coaching principals on how to use data to identify targets for improvement and giving principals the chance to learn from one another, district leaders created the system capacity for collaborative inquiry between the central office and school administrators. They had made it safe to focus on challenges without blaming.

Trust is maintained when district administrators often reinforce the purposes and norms of inquiry-based improvement. For instance, Sanger's associate superintendent opened the 2012 Principal Summit with these words to the three secondary school principals presenting that day (with an audience of over twenty district staff and visitors gathered in the boardroom):

> There are three things we want to do in today's Summit. (1) Assess our effectiveness on the basis of results, not on intentions. (2) Learn; learning is

our fundamental purpose, and we're willing to scrutinize our practices to do it. (3) Work together. Remember: none of us knows what we all know. Remember that this is about building our capacity. That is what we are here today to do.

Evidence-based dialogue between school leaders and district administrators and staff builds a shared understanding of specific problems to be addresses in each school, consensus on how the central office will support improvement, and mutual accountability for success.

In districts that have reached a tipping point in the administrative culture, principals became leaders in bringing teachers along as partners in inquiry-based improvement. Principals and teachers eventually took for granted that decisions must be based on evidence. A Long Beach elementary school principal put it this way: "We all live by the data, because that's how we know what's working."[10] A Sanger high school teacher described the change process for his course team in these terms: "We moved beyond comfort issues 3–4 years ago . . . We're not concerned any more about who [which teacher] did well, but what to do about the students. What's happened is that our scores on common assessments are coming to be more similar over the years."[11] Through district leaders' clear vision and modeling, teachers and administrators across the schools in each of these districts became convinced that strategic, data-based inquiry was *the* district reform approach and that they could sink their teeth into the hard work of doing it well to continuously improve their students' learning.

By leading change through norms of professionalism, the central office administrators gradually shifted district authority relationships away from top-down, bureaucratic control and compliance toward collaboration and mutual accountability focused on improving student success. Principals' and teachers' perceptions of the district changed when they saw administrators and staff consistently using evidence to make decisions about how to respond to schools' needs and supporting rather than blaming them for struggles to improve. Over the years mutual trust and accountability developed in these districts, and they became "nested" inquiry communities with strong track records of steady improvement in student achievement.

STAYING THE COURSE

Amid federal and state accountability pressures to keep improving student achievement, districts are being barraged with programs and change approaches that promise to bring gains. The solutions include "evidence-based" curricula, teacher training in content pedagogy, merit pay, charter schools, portfolios of schools, school restart and other turnaround designs, and myriad privatization schemes. Although data-based decision making may be on the rise as a school reform strategy, because of its link to federal criteria for improvement under NCLB and in spite of its earlier association with soft inquiry initiatives, this approach is not yet privileged in federal or major foundation policy and funding.

As the bandwagons of education reform roll on, district administrators are continually faced with the decision of what to buy into, what investment will improve student learning and success. Most opt for a patchwork of programs and initiatives that seem worthwhile and/or can bring external funding. In keeping with the idea of adopting best practices, district leaders and their private support organizations are on the lookout for signs of what works. Under the gun, many feel the need to be on the cutting edge with programs and practices that are getting the most buzz in the moment. These dynamics keep district reform in a constant state of churn and stack the cards against the success of any of the reforms. On top of this, district personnel and educators often grow cynical about the promise of a particular reform strategy and possibility of making significant school improvement, being fed up with a seemingly endless parade of reforms and losing patience for sticking with any one of them.

Yet schools that take on the challenge of developing teachers' capacity for strategic inquiry need steady support from their district, and their work is derailed if the district adopts reform strategies that pull them in a different direction. Schools' progress stalls, too, if principal turnover brings in someone who lacks the will or skill to sustain teacher teams' progress on strategic inquiry. Districts need a developmental understanding of schools' progress in order to be strategic about bringing innovations into the system. They can use benchmarks to track where a school or teacher team is in its capacity to sustain strategic inquiry and select a limited number of advanced teams to pilot promising innovations. For example, in preparing for the CCSS, New York City selected teacher teams identified as advanced on strategic inquiry to pilot instruction and assessments in particular content areas, a strategy to avoid pulling more novice teams off the track of developing robust inquiry practice. In piloting new approaches to English learner development (ELD) instruction, Sanger formed a task force of the principals of three elementary schools with a majority of English language learners who worked together for a year on developing new assessments and instructional responses, a strategy that avoided disrupting teacher teams' work and resulted in new, evidence-based resources to support their success with English learners.

Figure 6.2 captures the vision of a district culture of continuous improvement and the shifts entailed in getting there. A district that makes

FIGURE 6.2   Leading change toward district-wide strategic inquiry

District outcome	From . . .	To . . .
Widespread commitment to the vision and ownership of strategic inquiry	Mandating implementation of the model in terms of specific routines	Creating opportunities for principals and teachers to learn strategic inquiry principles and see evidence of success with students

Modeling strategic inquiry for district decisions |
| Collaborative, evidence-based decision making at all system levels | Using summative data to hold teachers and schools accountable for implementing routines and/or meeting targets for student test scores

Culture of blame and fear | Using formative data to focus and evaluate district decisions and to identify and respond to each school's improvement needs

Culture of support, trust, learning, and mutual accountability |
| Sustained focus on inquiry-based reform in face of external policy demands and reform ideas | Adopting multiple reform approaches tied to specific external policies and grants, with specialized offices and staff to enforce school compliance | Responding to external polices and grant opportunities strategically to maintain coherence with inquiry-based reform |

CHAPTER 7

Bringing Leadership Certification Programs on Board

School leadership certification programs can either advance or inhibit local capacity for inquiry-based improvement. Most programs do not equip leaders with the knowledge and skills they need to lead collaborative, evidence-based improvement, yet districts depend on them for their administrative pipeline.[1] At best, the graduates need additional training to lead and support strategic inquiry in their schools; at worst, they work at cross purposes by pushing a different approach to school improvement.

Although most states provide wide flexibility in how university programs organize to meet the state requirements (hours, curriculum, etc.), creating an aligned program is a significant and largely untapped opportunity to drive school improvement. Districts committed to strategic inquiry as an approach to continuous improvement might create partnerships with local feeder programs to redesign the training. Universities stand to benefit by improving the leadership skills of their graduates, getting additional resources from district partners, and demonstrating their school-level impact, as new state data systems and accountability policies will increasingly require.[2]

However, aligning a school leadership credentialing program with strategic inquiry is no small feat. It involves challenging the deeply entrenched practices and habits that sustain current programs. It means shifting long-standing traditions of curriculum and instruction in school leadership preparation and assumptions about the resources it takes to build an effective program.

To illustrate what it takes to bring about these program shifts, we describe the evolution of one program—the Scaffolded Apprenticeship Model at Baruch College, which parented strategic inquiry as a school reform model—and its investment in developing instructor/facilitator skills.[3] To assess how it paid off, we describe how its graduates have improved their schools and what they do differently because of what they learned. For those who may wish to grow such a program at home, we highlight core issues a design team is likely to confront.

THE ORIGINS AND EVOLUTION OF THE SCAFFOLDED APPRENTICESHIP MODEL

The idea for SAM was sparked in 2002 when Liz Gewirtzman, a faculty member in educational leadership in the School of Public Affairs at Baruch College and a cocreator with Sandra Stein and others of the Aspiring Leaders Program (ALP), reviewed evidence that an intensive, multiyear principal leadership development initiative in San Diego Public Schools had benefited elementary schools but failed to pay off in high schools.[4] The question was why. The answer from research on high schools was that decisions about instruction are made in the units closest to instruction, such as subject departments, so leadership development to improve student achievement in high schools would need to be broader and deeper than a principal initiative.[5]

Gewirtzman, who had recently agreed to design an administrator preparation program specifically for high schools, was struck by the need for deep, broad leadership for improving high schools in particular and suddenly wondered if preparing teams, rather than individuals, could make the needed difference.[6] "If research supports the need for distributed leadership," she wondered, "why are universities preparing individuals rather than teams?" The ALP program had prioritized teams to the extent possible with individual applicants. Students conducted most of their course-work as members of cross-school teams. Because they came from different schools, however, the problems they worked on together were simulated rather than real. Gewirtzman wondered how leadership preparation *and* actual school improvement might be enhanced if the applicant was a school team—particularly in large high schools, where siloed subject department cultures had proven notoriously resistant to reform.

She brought this question to Ron Chaluisan and Bob Hughes at New Visions for Public Schools, who were wrestling with how best to develop a leadership pipeline for their new small high schools. Chaluisan added his notion of a "nested apprenticeship" (teachers would be released part-time to apprentice as assistant principals, and assistant principals would be released part-time to apprentice as principals), and a plan for a partnership experiment in leadership preparation was born. In 2005 Gewirtzman, Chaluisan, and Nell Scharff Panero (then Scharff, who joined Baruch in 2004) launched SAM I, the pilot (then called the High School Leadership Development Program), with teams from four NYC public high schools, two large and two small.[7] The initial curriculum drew heavily on ALP and lessons learned from the first year of the newly formed New York City Leadership Academy, where Sandra Stein had become academic dean and where Gewirtzman was the lead facilitator.[8] But the program was distinctive in that the applicant was a school-based team; the principal was a member of both the school team and the facilitator team, helping design and teach program curriculum; and it included a school-based apprenticeship. The program began with a six-week summer intensive session that used simulated school problems to focus teams' assignments.

In SAM I and each subsequent iteration (see figure 7.1 for an overview of program iterations) lessons learned led to design improvements and eventually to the streamlined model that is strategic inquiry. In the pilot, several key lessons informed design changes:

- With the school team as the unit of preparation, simulations were no longer needed to ground the work; actual school problems were more immediate and complex, and working on them from the start would accelerate participants' learning and school improvement. This led to abandoning the simulation-based summer intensive as the launch for the program.

• Teams had tremendous difficulty moving from data analysis to action to improve learning for a group of struggling students in their school. The struggle of all four teams to take action in an action-research assignment given in the third of four semesters led to its becoming the initial, organizing task in subsequent iterations.

• Program leaders could not assume that team members knew instruction well. It became evident that SAM's curriculum needed to address instructional fundamentals such as lesson design (clear quality objectives, alignment of lesson elements with objectives, checks for understanding, etc.) as a prerequisite for their work in peer coaching and supervision assignments.

SAM II launched with the action-research task moved up front, but it was still a surprise to program leaders to learn just how difficult it was—and how much time and careful scaffolding it would take—to ensure that a team was effective in carrying out evidence-based improvement cycles. The notion of inquiry-based improvement as the driver across all semes-

FIGURE 7.1   SAM iterations at Baruch College, 2005–2013

SAM iteration	Years	Number of cohorts*	Number of schools	Number of students
SAM I	2005–2006	1	4	19
SAM II	2006–2007	4	12	100
SAM III**	2007–2011	11	36	155
SAM Citywide	2011–2013	3	40	54

*There was one SAM facilitator per cohort.
**SAM III involved four iterations that overlapped in time: SAM III(a) had five cohorts; III(b) had four cohorts; III(c) had two cohorts.

ters emerged and crystallized in this second iteration, along with the other essential lesson of getting small. As program facilitators became increasingly skilled in identifying what exactly was most difficult in the action-research task, they discovered that teams were simply not having success unless they focused on a manageable number of students and diagnosed precisely where learning for those students was breaking down. Getting small was the key, SAM facilitators discovered, in moving students (and later systems) and in shifting the hearts and minds of the participants along the way.

In the third and subsequent iterations, program designers foregrounded and better articulated the role of systems in the model as a whole.[9] Systems thinking had always been fundamental to the program's design for strategic inquiry. However, questions from participants and others about how getting so small could possibly make the needed big difference prompted program designers to refine and better communicate the model's systems orientation from the start.[10] At first, SAM designers and facilitators were likely to describe strategic inquiry phases in a linear fashion: move students, then systems, then colleagues. In later iterations, Phases I and II were presented as interconnected from the start. The core work of skill-gap identification in Phase I remained the same: diagnose skill gaps and close them. But participants' understanding of how doing so informed a larger, systemic goal (to illuminate particular system flaws to be improved) was different.

Other changes over time reflected the shifting context within which SAM operated. When the program began, there were no formal inquiry teams in New York City. By the fourth iteration, entering participants were likely to be familiar with district data systems, which were improving each year, and to have served at least nominally on a collaborative team. Some had negative experiences on a dysfunctional school team, but on the whole the district push and support for evidence-based collaboration accelerated what was possible in the SAM program.

In 2011, after the grant supporting New Visions' schools in SAM III had ended, Baruch launched SAM Citywide, an administrative credentialing program grounded in strategic inquiry for individual teachers who are part of a school-based team.[11] In the changed NYC context, schools were eager for support to improve their collaborative teams, which meant that individuals trained in strategic inquiry could be a potentially powerful lever for team and thus school improvement. From the program perspective, individual participants could carry out team assignments back in their schools. In this current model, participants work in two teams simultaneously: their Baruch team (comprised of participants across schools), where they learn strategic inquiry, and their home school team, where they apply what they learn. Assignments for both use the team structure to accelerate student achievement. Cross-school team members are collectively held accountable first for moving a target population comprised of students from each of their schools and, second, for improving inquiry team performance at each home school. The team assignments are designed to create collective accountability for what would otherwise be a solitary task.

What emerged over time is a distilled program model that turns traditional school leadership preparation on its head. It challenges established norms for the unit of preparation, role of the curriculum, role of the instructor, nature of instructor preparation and development, and desired program outcomes. (See figure 7.2 for a summary of these shifts.) What began as a school leadership program through school improve-

FIGURE 7.2   Shifts entailed in creating a strategic inquiry–aligned program

Program element	From . . .	To . . .
Unit of preparation	Individual	Team
Curriculum and assignments	Fixed as set out in syllabus	Dynamic; adjusted in response to evidence of learning needs
Instructor's role	Deliver curriculum to individuals	Facilitate team inquiry
Instructor's preparation	Prior experience	Concurrent facilitator training (learning community)
Expected outcomes	Credentialed leadership candidates	Improved student achievement in participants' schools
	Meeting standard in broad leadership competencies	Strong strategic inquiry leadership

ment became more accurately described as a school improvement program through leadership development. The fundamental notion of what it means to develop leaders and the driving purpose of the program changed as well. Leaders are seen as those who act collectively and strategically from whatever position they hold to continuously drive improvement. The original goal—to deepen high school leadership—came to include creating a tipping point of change leaders with and without formal authority throughout and across the system as a whole.

DEVELOPING FACILITATOR CAPACITY: THE KEY TO PROGRAM SUCCESS

Instructing/Facilitating in a strategic inquiry–aligned program involves a steep learning curve, even for those who bring a wealth of experience to the role. Doing it well, even after internalizing the strategic inquiry core principles, requires ongoing support. One experienced facilitator described the biggest challenges as "navigating shifting paradigms at every level" and managing the resistance that doing so creates.

> We're shifting a paradigm for the teachers in terms of how they have to work in a dynamic way with their students. And we're shifting a paradigm in terms of how graduate school professors work with their students. As instructors, we come in thinking that the program and the curriculum should be fixed, but it's inherent in the program content that it has to be dynamic. Obviously, having the basic SAM principles down is what helps you to be dynamic. But it's always a struggle, because it creates incredible resistance from every party—the schools, the principals, the students. No one wants to be dynamic, because it's uncertain and anxiety producing.

The SAM program's considerable investment in facilitator training has been the key to its success and is a critical ingredient for any aligned program. While there is still more to learn about the nature of facilitator learning—what qualities are best brought to the role, which training components are most and least essential—our research grounds a rudimentary developmental framework for facilitator learning to effectively leverage and support school teams' strategic inquiry. The framework maps *beginning, intermediate,* and *advanced phases,* indicating the most pressing challenges and implications for training at each phase.

Facilitators in the beginning phase, who may be experienced content instruction coaches or coaches for a different improvement model, typically enter the work focused on teaching rather than learning, implementing the curriculum in a somewhat mechanistic, rule-bound fashion and seeing themselves as deliverers of a curriculum in the mold of a university professor. The biggest challenge for the beginning facilitator is recognizing the difference between a focus on teaching and learning and coming to understand strategic inquiry principles, strategies, and the facilitator role in light of this shift in focus.

As one new facilitator said to a SAM trainer, "The distinction you make between teaching and learning is false. After all, you can't have one without the other." From this vantage point, the strategic inquiry tasks don't quite make sense. It was confusing to him, for example, that Phase I prioritized skill-gap identification over immediate instruction in best practices that he thought would close them. The time spent getting small seemed to him less productive than teaching participants to implement the best of what was known. Because they are countercultural, being taught strategic inquiry principles is insufficient for learning them. Beginning facilitators need time to learn the theory and curriculum firsthand—to collaboratively design activities and assignments, norm participant work products and adjust curriculum and assignments in response, practice and receive feedback on facilitation moves—and by doing so to internalize core principles so facilitation can become strategic. Facilitators, like participants, come to strategic inquiry steeped in the current culture of schooling. They, like participants, need time and the ongoing support of a professional community to reorient themselves and to learn.

Facilitators in the intermediate phase have begun to shift from a focus on teaching to learning (students', teachers', their own) and toward a deeper understanding of the strategic inquiry foundational principles and theory of change. They are increasingly skilled in intervening strategically rather than by following the letter of the law. An intermediate facilitator is more able than a beginner to recognize and redirect team resistance, for instance, but they do so inconsistently. One intermediate facilitator recognized when a team, on its fourth comma diagnostic, needed to move on and was not derailed as a beginner may have been when the team said that in getting small they were doing just what the facilitator had asked. This same facilitator, however, was pulled off course by another team's insistence that they focus only on seniors. Afterward, in discussion with the facilitator team, the facilitator said she regretted this decision, that she'd felt pressure to comply with the team's report of what their principal wanted. In retrospect, she felt she'd lost an opportunity to fully develop the team's inquiry capacity and that the next time she would make a different decision.

Most challenging for the intermediate facilitator is feeling uprooted from old beliefs without being rerooted in the new. This middle ground is particularly unsettling for those who come to the role as experts in a different model of reform. Intermediate facilitators need the support of a collaborative team to validate their experience and to help them move through it. Discussions about particular facilitator moves like those described above—about why they made them, pros and cons, alternative options, etc.—are central in developing facilitators' capacity to make strategic decisions that advance particular teams' progress. In addition, facilitators at this stage continue to learn new strategic inquiry content (applying principles of moving students to moving systems and colleagues) as they engage it deeply in preparation for teaching and in the actual teaching of it to participants.

Facilitators in the advanced phase have become solidly grounded in a focus on learning and are skilled at intervening strategically in alignment with deep principles of strategic inquiry. They are less likely than those in earlier phases to be pulled off task, yet they are still vulnerable, as the earlier quote by an experienced facilitator makes clear. Collaboration remains critical for grounding them and to ensure continued learning, for both facilitators themselves and for the program as a whole. Intermediate and advanced facilitators apply cycles of inquiry to learn and improve when they are stuck. One group of facilitators, for example, noticed that participants were struggling to meet standard in their peer coaching assignment, that they were not able to identify and/or to push their colleagues to create clear and measurable learning objectives in peer coaching conversations. The facilitators assumed (as is the strategic inquiry stance) that the participants' not meeting standard was a reflection of their teaching and that they needed to learn more about how exactly the assignment and/or their instruction needed to improve. To do so, they created diagnostics; in this case, they had participants annotate their coaching transcripts so that they could learn more about participant thinking that informed the coaching moves. Greater understanding of participant thinking led to different teaching decisions by facilitators, which led more participants to meet standard on the assignment.[12]

Equally important—and essential for program quality—facilitators at all developmental levels continually evaluate the extent to which curriculum and instruction provide participants with what they need to meet the program's specific school improvement goals. The goals themselves remain solid; participants need to move students, move systems, and move colleagues. The places and ways in which participants get stuck, however, provide critical information that facilitators must evaluate and respond to. At times, program curriculum and instruction need to improve. Other times, the surrounding context has changed, and what worked in the past is no longer matched well with current needs. Time for all levels of facilitators to continually evaluate evidence of the impact of assignments on participant learning and actual school improvement is the mechanism to ensure tight alignment with actual school improvement needs. With their deep knowledge of core strategic inquiry principles, advanced facilitators are especially skilled in designing adaptations to context that do not violate these core principles.

This considerable investment in facilitator learning is unusual in university and school reform settings, and we've noticed that it is often the first thing to be cut when budgets are tight. However, evidence from our research and practice makes clear that facilitator training is crucial for achieving strong results for participants and thus is central to the success of the certification program. Our preliminary research suggests that well-trained facilitators typically move from the beginning to the developing phase within one semester and to the advanced phase by the end of the fourth and final semester. Available, though scant, evidence regarding the trajectory of facilitator learning suggests that training for new facilitators in a certification model should include one full day per week through an entire cycle of the program. For those who have taught one full iteration, participation in training one full day per month may be sufficient to ensure that the program evolves in response to changing contexts and learning needs.

BENEFITS OF ALIGNED PROGRAMS, NEAR AND LONG TERM

Given the considerable investment required to shift existing programs to align with strategic inquiry, why is doing so worth the effort? The benefits are twofold: the particular habits and skills a certified leader brings to a school and the impact on host principals and schools during the experience of building a cadre of teacher-leaders trained in strategic inquiry. Our evidence comes from graduates of the SAM program.

Administrator Skills

Program graduates who have taken on new administrator roles tend to lead differently—specifically, with a focus on student learning and by prioritizing inquiry to build coherence, develop capacity, and continuously improve student performance. They apply inquiry to varying school improvement problems, instructional and noninstructional; put feedback systems in place to inform ongoing, evidence-based adjustments; and, most distinctively, get small to make improvement manageable and strategic and thus effective. In doing so, they help teachers come to own improvement efforts rather than experience them as imposed from above. These administrators become, essentially, strategic inquiry facilitators working on the inside.

Hillcrest's Dan Scanlon, a strategic inquiry-trained principal, used various forms of inquiry as his core improvement strategy from the start. He launched an inquiry team of administrators to improve dire attendance rates, including focusing on a strategically selected target population to make the work manageable and to yield results. He simultaneously implemented two other forms of inquiry to drive instruction improvement: the first, of a down-and-dirty variety, focused on moving select tenth through twelfth graders to pass needed Regents exams as quickly as possible; the second, a slower, deeper form, focused on diagnosing literacy skill gaps for ninth graders and refining development of and teacher capacity in a new literacy curriculum. In addition, Scanlon brought low-inference transcripts as a core leadership tool to his cabinet, teaching instructional supervisors to create them and use them in coaching and supervisory conversations. "More than anything, these transcripts really helped my teachers to improve," Scanlon said when asked how he used low-inference transcripts in his prior position as an assistant principal and why he brought them to his new role as principal. "It's one thing to be told what you need to improve; it's a whole other thing to see it for yourself."

As mentioned earlier, SAM graduate Dina Zoleo used the getting small approach and the inquiry process as an assistant principal to lead teachers in her department to identify for themselves the skills she had come to learn students were missing and thus to build buy-in for a new skill-based curriculum and to raise the effectiveness of teachers in her department. "When we create a consistent, skill-based curriculum," Zoleo explained, "the level of all my teachers rises. Curriculum is huge." Having shifted her focus from teaching to learning as a SAM participant, Zoleo, when she became assistant principal of the same department in which she'd trained, pushed that focus department wide. "We used be a really strong content department," she explained. "Now, we still teach content, and our kids know the content better. But we've shifted to being focused on teaching the kids first and skills along with content. Every week we get together and look at evidence to see whether our kids got both the skill and the content. And if they didn't get it, we try again." The biggest shift in strategic inquiry–trained administrators' approach is their relentless focus on adjusting practice in light of evidence of student learning. They model this practice and develop it in those they supervise.

The Benefit for Host Schools and Leaders

Most persuasive for aligning certification programs with strategic inquiry, perhaps, is evidence from the SAM evaluation that commitment to the model (schools sending multiple teams for training over at least three years) results in significant improvement in student outcomes; these schools brought more struggling students on track to graduation than similar schools who did not participate. Also significant are the shifts in practice, beliefs, and systems beyond those directly touched by the program.[13] In other words, there is strong evidence of school-wide improvement.

Evidence from our evaluation suggests that changes in beliefs, practices, and efficacy accrue to host principals as well, particularly principals in the early iterations and/or those who invested heavily in strategic inquiry as a strategy for reform. Deirdre DeAngelis and Steve Duch, for example, two veteran large-school principals, speak readily about the impact of their schools' participation in SAM on their own thinking and leadership. Duch credits SAM with reigniting his passion for the profession and ensuring his own and his school's continued growth.

> In year eight of my principalship [and thirtieth year in the district], when I got involved in SAM I, I could have very easily gone on autopilot. All the big problems in the school had really been dealt with: we were a midperforming school; we were not appearing on anybody's radar list. It would have been very easy for this school to stay the way it was and not change. I see that many of my colleagues chose that path. But having gotten involved with SAM really kept me on the cutting edge of school reform. If I were not to have been involved in SAM, I think it would have been a detriment to my evolution as a school leader . . . The program's mission was building a new cadre of school leaders, but also building the capacity of the current building leader as well.

When explaining the turnaround history at her school to a group of visitors recently, DeAngelis said, "All the changes you see here are related to inquiry. In fact, every change we make in this building now is based on data." This shift to across-the-board evidence-based decision making is key to what strategic inquiry–trained leaders do differently. "We used to bundle up the Regents exams and leave them sitting in a classroom. We never looked at the results," explained DeAngelis. "Not anymore. Now my assistant principals can't wait to get their hands on them and do an item analysis. We don't even wait for the Regents anymore. We give mock assessments and analyze them all the time, so we're never surprised."

Furthermore, a deep understanding of the principles and processes of strategic inquiry provides an experienced principal with a powerful tool (getting small) with which to build coherence among what may otherwise be experienced as competing or contradictory initiatives. DeAngelis helped her staff make sense of a new teacher effectiveness mandate, for example, by first selecting one of the six dimensions on a potentially overwhelming rubric as that year's area of focus and then by suggesting that each teacher identify the smallest, aligned element within that broader dimension on which to focus. Instead of working on all six dimensions in the rubric or even on one full dimension, she suggested that they create a baseline and track improvement in the smallest element possible. In doing so she was able to (1) make an otherwise overwhelming new initiative manageable; (2) maintain coherence both in terms of process (inquiry) and of content (the particular dimension she selected was consistent with other areas of focus); and (3) most importantly, perhaps, she was able to maintain a growth approach and ensure quality in assessing growth. Getting small helped to ensure that growth would be judged according to evidence of a cause-effect relationship between changes in teacher practice and improved student performance rather than by changes in teacher practice alone.

Not all teams have principals that engage with strategic inquiry to the extent described above, but these examples illustrate how, if designed to support principal and school involvement, the model can be an immediate lever for whole-school development and improvement.

Leadership Pipeline

During the program and after graduation, participants in strategic inquiry–aligned programs take on existing teacher leadership roles or new ones that emerge as inquiry spreads and/or as an outgrowth of what is learned through the process. In general we have found that teacher-leaders who got small in their own training lead their colleagues more effectively than those who did not, moving back and forth between getting small and getting big as needed to yield the most improvement. They understand the underlying purpose of getting small and are therefore less likely to fall into the common traps of staying too vague to learn something new or too small to make a big enough difference.

New teacher leadership roles emerge as well that tap the particular interests and skills of those who may not yet wish to leave the classroom. At New Dorp, for example, the success of a schoolwide writing initiative in a few departments cultivated interest in and the need for additional support in other departments. Toni-Ann Vroom, a strategic inquiry veteran who was especially passionate about and skilled in the writing strategies and was well respected by colleagues, emerged to fill a newly created position of cross-content writing coach. She did not want a formal administrative position but was happy to take on a new role that allowed her to support curricular and instructional improvement while remaining a classroom teacher. She was particularly effective as a teacher in this role, since learning to integrate literacy into high school content was threatening for some teachers, and the collegial, nonpositional relationship fostered an openness to learning the new strategies.

The demonstrated success of strategic inquiry training programs in improving student outcomes and school culture while developing a cadre of leaders at all levels prepared to lead inquiry-based improvement is the best evidence that an investment in shifting current programs is worthwhile.

DESIGNING AN ALIGNED PROGRAM

To be aligned with strategic inquiry, a school leadership program must be organized to support team success in a task-based curriculum grounded in the model's three inquiry phases and theory of change. It must also provide substantial time for facilitator training and support. These features imply several key shifts from what is typical.

FIGURE 7.3   Design decisions associated with core shifts

Program element	Shift to . . .	Associated design decision
Unit of preparation	Team	How to recruit teams/compose cohorts
Curriculum and assignments	Dynamic; adjusted in response to evidence of learning needs	How to align curriculum with strategic inquiry tasks
Instructor's role	Facilitate team inquiry	How to select instructors
Instructor's preparation	Concurrent facilitator training (learning community)	How to train and support instructors
Expected outcomes	Improved student achievement in participants' schools	How to measure strong inquiry leadership
	Strong strategic inquiry leadership	

Even for a design team that has bought into these core shifts, there are decisions associated with each shift that will impact the shape of the resulting design and that must be addressed in light of the program's driving purposes, access to schools and participants, and available resources (see figure 7.3).[14]

Shift to the Team as the Unit of Preparation

Designers of a program aligned with strategic inquiry must decide how to recruit school teams (applicants) and the ideal cohort composition.[15] The program can either recruit teams from across schools, to create a cross-school cohort, or from within a school or network, to create a school- or network-based cohort. Advantages of a cross-school cohort include diversity (the strategic inquiry stance has been "the more diversity, the better," in terms of school level, size, philosophy, etc.) and the ability to adhere to more rigorous admissions standards, in a traditional sense. However, a program may accept some students with lower grade point averages than would otherwise be expected if they decide to prioritize creating a critical mass of leaders within one school. This may be seen as a disadvantage in particular settings or as a challenge to secure changed admission requirements. However, the advantages include that a critical mass of change agents within one school or district—particularly when the teams and the approach are endorsed by current leaders—is a powerful lever for actual school improvement. This has proven especially true in large high schools. Where school- or district-based cohorts exist, principals are typically highly involved, and it's often possible to conduct the program on-site and, if resources are available, to augment regular instruction with other kinds of support, such as additional time on site by the strategic inquiry facilitator/instructor and/ or opportunities for participants to visit each other's schools. Program designers should make decisions about the ideal model in alignment with the driving program priority—to certify star leaders in a traditional sense or to improve particular schools or districts as quickly as possible.

Shift to a Task-Based Curriculum

For those adapting existing programs to strategic inquiry or creating a parallel program where a state-approved sequence of courses already exists, we recommend beginning this process by mapping existing courses to strategic inquiry's basic phases and tasks (see table 7.4). The map can then be expanded to include core assignments, standards each assignment is intended to develop and test, aligned learning objectives, and core skills and habits of mind to be developed. It may be helpful to keep in mind that, unlike in a model based on discrete courses, the skills and habits developed across strategic inquiry phases spiral, with the idea that they are developed over time with increasing complexity and depth (see appendix E). Note as well that some required courses and/or course content may not map to strategic inquiry tasks, such as with some law and finance topics. This material can be taught in stand-alone courses or integrated into existing coursework where it fits best.

Shift in the Instructor's Role and Training

Given that a strategic inquiry–aligned model entails a different conception of the instructor's role than is typical and that it involves substantial

FIGURE 7.4   Map of existing courses to strategic inquiry phases and tasks

	Organizing school improvement/ leadership development task (and aligned strategic inquiry phase)	Courses/Credits (24 total for School Building Leadership Certification)
Semester 1	Identify high-leverage skill gap and move struggling students (Phase I)	School Leadership and Organizational Management (3) Instructional Leadership (3)
Semester 2	Understand how the school as a system produces the outcomes for the target students; act strategically to improve an instructional decision system (Phase II)	Instructional Leadership in Educational Organizations (3) Legal and Policy Issues for the School Leader (3)
Semester 3	Continue to improve identified system and lead colleagues outside original team to move students and move system (Phases II & III)	School Leadership in the Community (3) School Finance and Budgeting (3)
Semester 4	Work at sustainability: embed in structures and decision rules processes for continual adjustments in response to evidence of student learning needs (Phases II & III)	Internship and Seminar I (3) Internship and Seminar II (3)

time for training, it may or may not be possible to staff an aligned program with university faculty. Program designers should secure additional resources to ensure that instructors (whether from inside or outside the university) are paid in accordance with the realistic time demands of this model. Designers need to ensure one full day per week (for new instructors in the program) for facilitator collaboration and support. This is a core design element; it's essential for a certification-bearing program to be considered aligned with strategic inquiry.

Shift to Strategic Inquiry–Aligned Performance Standards

Most school leadership credentialing programs are either required to or elect to align course content with existing state standards. Programs in thirty-five states, including New York, for example, are required to align with Interstate School Leaders Licensure Consortium (ISLLC) standards that specify graduates' expected knowledge, dispositions, and skills in six key areas.[16] In many cases, as in New York, content on required state certification exams maps to these standards as well. A strategic inquiry–aligned program, however, has a more specific theory of change, approach, and set of expectations than typically specified in national- or state-level standards. Graduates of strategic inquiry–aligned programs will have demonstrated their ability to work collaboratively to improve outcomes for struggling students, to improve systems, and to lead colleagues in evidence-based improvements. The knowledge, dispositions, and skills they will have demonstrated are consistent with ISLLC and other general leadership standards but are more particular and performance based. Designers of strategic inquiry–aligned programs need to create measurable leadership outcome standards for participants and their program that make strategic inquiry the priority.

Although aligning certification-bearing school leadership programs with strategic inquiry requires additional resources and entails considerable challenges, failing to do so exacts a cost for graduates and the schools and students they serve. Districts can be critical consumers of and partners with the credentialing programs that feed leaders into their schools. Doing so can help ensure that all oars are pulling in the same direction. Evidence points to strategic inquiry as a promising model around which to organize a district-university partnership and offers a set of principles and design elements to guide this work.

Conclusion

Schools and districts across the nation are desperately in search of how best to dedicate their time, commitment, and resources to improve student achievement and meet the demands of the Common Core State Standards. In this book we offer a road map toward sustainable improvement—not a quick fix, because there is none. The model we offer steadily and dramatically improves student outcomes and school culture. It is grounded in the experiences of more than a hundred high schools and evidence from six years of evaluation. It's a set of design elements and principles—namely, the 4Ts of teams, targets, tasks, and training paired with the principle of getting small to get big results. Any school can make progress by adhering to the model; however, aligned district support and leader certification programs can stimulate, accelerate, and extend schools' progress.

We've argued that building a school's capacity to improve student achievement takes more than training educators in technical skills and routines of data use. Technical training for educators to become good at doing things that most of them never learned to do—like using data to identify student skill gaps—is essential but not enough. What's needed is a model designed to shift teachers' typical practices and mind-sets. Strategic inquiry leads teachers to recognize and challenge assumptions about why students struggle, about their ability to teach them, and about their role and efficacy as leaders of continuous improvement. In effect, schools become learning organizations.

Without repeating strategic inquiry's design and phases for team practice, we end with the big ideas that ground the model and that guide its adaptation in new contexts. They hark back to the theory of change and build on experiences of many teams and facilitators:

- The results that any school produces are based on its existing policies, instructional structures and practices, and professional culture. Therefore, changing outcomes means that these need to change.

- Schools are not all the same, so what needs to change cannot be specified in advance. Improvement depends on the capacity of school leaders and staff to diagnose what gets in the way of student success.

- Big change doesn't come about quickly or all at once across a school. Change starts small and strategically in ways that leverage shifts in "the way we do things here."

- Educators' beliefs about why students fail and whether and how teachers can make a difference change when they go through the process. Figuring out at a fine-grained level what students need to learn to be more successful and then seeing positive results after programmed changes makes all the difference.

- Getting teacher teams over the hurdles of working through successful inquiry cycles requires a skilled facilitator who understands and anticipates predictable resistance and struggles.

Nothing short of systematically and strategically targeting those aspects of school culture that impede progress will turn the tides of high student failure rates in American schools. No recipe for school redesign or schemes to pressure or entice educators to work harder at what they know how to do will create the conditions necessary for continuous improvement: teacher collaboration, shared accountability, evidence use, and broad school leadership. And developing these conditions is especially urgent now, when most of the nation's states are rolling out more rigorous standards for student performance. Without teachers working together to diagnose and close student achievement gaps, these gaps will broaden rather than close. Through strategic inquiry, the nation's schools and districts could achieve unprecedented results.

Low-Inference Transcripts

WHAT ARE LOW-INFERENCE TRANSCRIPTS?

Low-inference transcripts (LITs) are detailed scripts of what takes place in a class—just the facts, what a teacher and students say and do. They are designed to filter out the inferences and assumptions observers typically make about what occurred and why. In doing so, they provide data for teachers to examine to see what occurred and discuss different ideas about why, to what effect, and next steps. A LIT of an entire lesson can illuminate important areas for analysis beyond those an observer may initially have selected. It allows for close, precise analysis of what occurred in particular lessons and promotes shared understanding of patterns in instruction across classrooms. LITs should be used to support investigation, not as a "gotcha" tool. Because sharing and analyzing evidence of actual practice is countercultural in most school settings, those wishing to implement LITs should proceed slowly and thoughtfully, with attention to building trust so their purpose can be realized.

HOW ARE THEY DIFFERENT FROM TYPICAL CLASSROOM OBSERVATION NOTES?

Typically classroom observers summarize what they see and hear with notes, tallies, or a combination of the two. Summaries can be useful and efficient, and we are not suggesting they should never be used. However, LITs can be more useful when the goal is to collaboratively make meaning of instruction and/or to develop a teacher's ability to make evidence-based meaning themselves. Unlike summaries—which include inferences about motivation without providing the evidence with which the inferences can be challenged—and tallies, which require up-front decisions about what's worth counting, LITs minimize up-front judgment and selection. They allow for interpretation after the fact by the observed teacher and/or in a collaborative, evidence-based back-and-forth exchange.

As an illustration, consider the summary of a lesson in relation to the low-inference description of part of the same lesson.

Observer summary
In this lesson the teacher uses a cartoon to reach and engage visual learners. The teacher has students define the concept of mimic in their own words and collectively create a definition.

Low-inference transcript of a portion of the lesson
Class: Living Environment (15 students, sitting in groups)
A cartoon is projected on a screen at the front of the room: a drawing of an elephant thinly disguised as a rhinoceros. The caption reads: Don't worry, according to the guide book we're dealing with a rhino mimic.
Assignment (written on the board): Do Now: Look at the cartoon and write down what you think a "mimic" is.
STUDENT 1: What does the cartoon say? I can't read the words.
TEACHER: *(Reading)* What is a mimic? Write what you think it means in your own words
STUDENT 1: *(Beginning to write)* A mimic tries to scare other animals.
TEACHER: How does it scare other animals?
STUDENT 1: It looks scary.
TEACHER: It makes itself look like something it's not. How?
STUDENT 1: Makes itself look big.
TEACHER: Student 2, can you read what you wrote?
STUDENT 2: *(Reading)* It tries to copy another animal.
TEACHER: In this cartoon, what is it trying to copy?
STUDENT 1: A rhinoceros.
TEACHER: So who can come up with a definition of a mimic? Student 3?
STUDENT 3: An animal that tries to copy . . . I don't know.

TEACHER: Good, we have the copy part. *(Writing on board and reading aloud)* "Mimic: An animal that copies another animal to . . ." Why? Does anyone have anything to add?

STUDENT 1: To scare other animals.

TEACHER: Right. *(Writing on board and reading aloud)* ". . . to increase its chance of survival."

If a number of different teachers were asked to analyze the evidence closely, they may or may not agree that this lesson is effective in engaging all students, or that students and the teacher collectively generate a definition. (A close reading of the LIT reveals that the teacher actually creates the definition and provides no evidence that the students know or understand it.) As this example illustrates, analysis of LITs helps to illuminate gaps between intended and actual curriculum—the gap between what teachers intend to teach and what students actually receive. In helping teachers gain this clear, shared understanding of actual learning conditions, LITs are crucial in generating grounded knowledge and energy for focused change.

HOW LONG DOES IT TAKE TO LEARN TO PRODUCE LITS?

Developing LIT muscle and skill (being fast and accurate enough to produce a trustworthy transcript, one the observed teacher would feel accurately reflects what happened in the lesson, without judgment) takes a bit of time and practice—but not as much as novice transcribers think. After generating two or three, most people can create a trustworthy transcript.

Where to Begin— Paragraph or Sentence?

Assess one body paragraph from each student using the chart on the following page.

1. Place a Y or N in each box.

2. Count the number of Ns for Categories A and B.

3. Start in the category where you have more Ns.

		Student 1	Student 2	Student 3	Student 4	Student 5	Student 6
A. Structure and content	Does the paragraph have one main idea?						
	Does every sentence support the main idea?						
	Are the sentences logically related to one another?						
	Are detail sentences elaborated with accurate detail?						
Total number of Ns							
B. Sentence skills	Are there sentences that correctly use the conjunctions but, because, so?						
	Are sentences varied in terms of sentence structure?						
	Are sentences varied in terms of language?						
	Are sentences mechanically correct (no run-ons or errors in capitalization)?						
Total number of Ns							

Note: This tool is designed to be used with Judith C. Hochman's *Teaching Basic Writing Skills.*

Tennis Chart

Purpose: To help a team

- Break down a learning goal into discrete, measurable steps
- Determine what to work on next
- Chart progress

Definition: A visual articulation of a hypothesis ("I believe that if X person got better at Y, this would lead to our larger goal. And, more specifically, that the component skills necessary to succeed at Y are a, b, c, d.")

Suggested steps for making a tennis chart:

1. Articulate the skill (tennis)
2. Articulate the subskill (serve)
3. Articulate the learning targets (ball toss, grip, etc.)
4. Indicate for each learning target/box √, X, or ?. In doing so, consider: How do I know this? What is my evidence and how good is it?

After doing all of this, make a decision: What learning target will I work on next and why? How will I know if it's been mastered? (Each learning target/box needs its own assessment, its own way of knowing if each student can do that precise thing.)

TENNIS EXAMPLE

Skill: Tennis

Subskill: Serve

Learning targets: Ball toss, grip, foot position

	Ball toss	Grip	Foot position
Student A	X	√	√
Student B	?	?	√
Student C	X	X	√

Key: X: has not mastered (according to evidence); ?: I don't know/I need more information; √: has mastered (according to evidence).

WRITING EXAMPLE

Skill: Expository essay

Subskill: Topic sentence and details

Learning targets: Distinguish general from specific statements; given a topic sentence, provide relevant details; given details, provide a topic sentence; eliminate irrelevant details

	Distinguish general from specific statements	Given a topic sentence, provide relevant details	Given details, provide a topic sentence	Eliminate irrelevant details
Student A	X	√	X	?
Student B	?	√	√	√
Student C	√	√	X	√

Phase III Rubric: School Team Assessment

Dimension	Poor (0–3)	Moderate (4–6)	High (7–10)
Level of principal support	Principal does not support collaboration or inquiry. If she does have teams, their support is for compliance only.	Principal supports inquiry and/or collaboration in a general sense but does not necessarily invest in teacher team development, authorize their decision making, or protect their time.	Principal values and communicates the value of inquiry and/or collaborative teams. She may or may not participate actively in the team.
Meeting regularity	Team does not meet or team meets but not frequently or regularly, and/or meetings are scheduled but not protected.	There is regular, scheduled time for team(s) to meet, at least monthly. If monthly, time is protected; if weekly, this time is somewhat but not fully prioritized/protected.	Team meets regularly, at least weekly. This is seen as a high priority, and time is only taken away in emergencies.
Team charge/ purpose	Purpose and charge of team is absent or unclear or unrelated to student learning.	Purpose/charge was made clear and is related to student learning, but all team members may not grasp or hold to this purpose consistently.	Purpose/charge was made clear and/or is clear among all team members and is strongly related to improving student learning. The team lives the purpose.

Dimension	Poor (0–3)	Moderate (4–6)	High (7–10)
Quality of talk	Talk is off task and/or involves complaining about students. Few teachers contribute meaningfully to the conversation. Conversation involves blaming students and/or their home lives.	Most talk in on task. Most participants are involved. Talk is generally about where student learning is breaking down or what teachers can do to try to improve learning for struggling students.	Talk is specific and precise. Most conversation is focused on identifying student learning gaps and/or or evidence of what practices work (or don't work) to close them.
Level of engagement	Team members are generally passive and/or compliant. Resistors' comments or behavior predominate or create a domino effect. Team members do not take risks or challenge each other.	Team members are willing to go along, even if not fully invested in or skilled in the process. There may be resistors or skeptics, but they do not dominate. At times conversation remains too "nice" to develop broad, deep engagement; but some risks are taken.	All or almost all team members are fully engaged. Team culture marginalizes/ neutralizes a resistor. Team does not shy away from productive conflict to develop and sustain deep, broad engagement.
Use of evidence	Conversation is not grounded in evidence. Decisions made are not evidence based.	Conversation and decisions are somewhat evidence based, or, they are evidence-based but the quality of evidence used is weak.	Evidence of student learning needs or impact of instructional practices drives conversations and decisions. Evidence used and inferences based on the evidence are high quality.
Accountability for results	No decisions are made and/or they are made but not followed up on. Team members do not hold each other accountable for follow-through or results.	Decisions may be made but may be inconsistently followed up on. Team members sometimes, but inconsistently, hold each other accountable for a lack of follow-through and/or a focus on results.	Team members generally make agreements and follow through. There is a results-orientation, and team members challenge members who fail to follow through on agreements.

Note: This tool can be used by a strategic inquiry facilitator to identify and track team development in Phase I or by teams in their work moving colleagues in Phase III. It provides a sense of the developmental arc of team functioning in strategic inquiry.

Strategic Inquiry Skills

1. Applies inquiry flexibly to push learning
   a. Sets aligned learning goals (focused on student/adult/system learning, evidence based, strategic, measurable, challenging but achievable)
   b. Generates or collects aligned evidence and makes decisions based on this evidence
   c. Manages when and how to get small
   d. Acts in iterative, evidence-based cycles
   e. Pushes for clarity; identifies jargon and doesn't accept it without questioning it
2. Presents evidence-based information clearly
   a. Is able to wade through data to select information that supports key points
   b. Takes outliers and disconfirming information into account; does not distort the data
   c. Creates data displays that organize and illuminate key patterns
   d. Illuminates patterns with a human story
   e. Uses summary and detail effectively to emphasize key points for intended purpose and audience

3. Uses collaboration effectively
   a. Seeks and makes use of Wisdom of Crowds
   b. Knows when and how to attend to team dynamics and process in service of results
   c. Holds others and oneself accountable to agreements
   d. Can effectively engage in conflict to ensure that all ideas are heard and can push through conflict to reach the best decisions
   e. Takes risks in public and can learn publicly from mistakes

4. Leads change
   a. Demonstrates action orientation from both positional and non-positional authority
   b. Analyzes system design and predicts system behavior
   c. Seeks and identifies leverage points
   d. Identifies problems to solve versus dilemmas to manage and matches strategies accordingly
   e. Considers inter- and intrapersonal factors in the change process and looks for evidence of impact of own behavior

Meeting standard on the above criteria and dimensions certifies that a person is ready to lead colleagues as a strategic inquiry facilitator. These criteria could form the backbone of outcome standards in a leadership credentialing program. They are aligned with, but more specific than ISLCC standards, focusing in on skills needed to lead change via strategic inquiry.

Notes

Introduction

1. Children First Intensive was part of NYC's move to school autonomy and accountability reform begun in 2006–2007 under the Bloomberg-Klein administration. It featured inquiry teams and the model for inquiry created by the SAM program, beginning with a pilot in a subset of schools and launched systemwide in 2007–2008. By 2009–2010 the city's department of education asked schools to involve most teachers in inquiry teams focused on improving the achievement of struggling students. The expectation of inquiry teams has persisted, with less prescription of inquiry practice.

2. This finding is consistent with evidence reported by Gallimore and colleagues that the practices effective inquiry teams discover work to bring new learning for struggling students run counter to those often seen as "best practice." They describe changes in practice that work to improve learning for students and make the cause-effect relationship so visible that teachers get "on the path to continual learning." And "While these improvements were regarded by teachers as worthwhile for teaching something better, and a change they intended to continue, they seldom matched teaching practices aspired to by some critics of traditional instructional practices" (547). Ronald Gallimore, Bradley A. Ermeling, William M. Saunders, and Claude Goldenberg, "Moving the Learning of Teaching Closer to Practice: Teacher Education Implications of School-Based Inquiry Teams," *Elementary School Journal* 109, no. 5 (2009): 537–552.

Part I

1. The philosophical roots of inquiry trace back to John Dewey, who envisioned school as a place where people reflect on and learn from their experience, and were picked up by Robert J. Schaefer in *The School as a Center of Inquiry* (New York: Harper-Collins, 1967) and by Donald Schon in *The Reflective Practitioner* (New York: Basic Books, 1983). Although inquiry found little traction in school systems until recently, a teacher research movement carried the idea through teacher networks that have been nurtured and studied by university scholars. See Marilyn Cochran-Smith and Susan L. Lytle, "Relationships of Knowledge and Practice: Teacher Learning in Communities," *Review of Research in Education* 24, no 2 (1999): 249–305.

2. The Annenberg Challenge initiative (1995–2006) promoted inquiry-based school reform and provided generous funding to several large districts. Evaluation research across the Annenberg sites found little evidence of impact. Few schools involved in the initiative developed the kind of inquiry culture needed to significantly improve student achievement. The Stanford Center for Research on the Context of Teaching (CRC) evaluated the Bay Area School Reform Collaborative, funded for ten years by Annenberg Challenge and Hewlett Foundation grants, and found that its cycle of inquiry schema and general guidelines were too vague to create new teacher practice that could shift teachers' thinking and school culture.

3. This was the story across the school systems that bought into the principle of inquiry-based reform in this earlier era: efforts were overly general and overwhelmed by top-down approaches to improvement. The models lacked a design for inquiry that could get to the heart of student learning needs and provide a plan for leadership development. Much of the learning for inquiry resided in administrators' heads, and the individuals charged with facilitating inquiry had no model to follow and little training.

Chapter 1

1. Strategic inquiry's theory of teams draws on Heifetz and Linsky's distinction between technical and adaptive change; Cuban's distinction between a problem that can be solved and a dilemma that can only be "managed;" and Surowiecki's notion that, under certain conditions, teams are wiser than any individual member. Ronald A. Heifetz and Marty Linsky, *Leadership on the Line* (Cambridge, MA: Harvard Education Press, 2002); Larry Cuban, *How Can I Fix It: Finding Solutions and Managing Dilemmas; An Educator's Roadmap* (New York: Teachers College Press, 2001); James Surowiecki, *The Wisdom of Crowds* (New York: Doubleday, 2004).

2. In early iterations of strategic inquiry in New York City the phases were likely to be rolled out in a linear fashion: first teams move students, then systems, then colleagues. This made sense given that teams were not yet commonplace in the city's public schools. However, in more recent and current iterations, it's more likely that teams first move students, then move colleagues (i.e., lead inquiry or other sorts of teams, since they are usually on one already), and then lead system improvement.

3. In 2008 and 2009 the evaluation team surveyed teachers in school teams with facilitators who differed in their strategic inquiry training and intensity of team support. Both years teachers rated their team on functioning with a focus on results, leadership for data-based improvement in their immediate teaching environment (department or SLC in large schools), and their facilitator's support of the team's inquiry work. Statistical analysis of these ratings for thirty-eight schools found a strong positive effect of facilitator support on team functioning over time, as well as a strong effect of team functioning on leadership for data-based improvement in 2009, after controlling for 2008 levels. In short, the longitudinal survey data show a powerful effect of facilitator support on a team's progress on strategic inquiry.

Chapter 2

1. The external evaluation was conducted by a team (led by Joan Talbert) from the Stanford University Center for Research on the Context of Teaching (CRC) from 2005–2006 through 2010–2011. Research methods for tracking change included annual teacher surveys in the roughly eighty New Visions schools and four-year case studies of twelve schools selected for their contrasts in strategic inquiry commitment (with and without teams being trained through the SAM credential program) and school size. This sample included schools in all five NYC boroughs. The case studies collected data through, in addition to teacher surveys, quarterly on-site interviews with the principal, facilitator(s), and teacher-leaders (including SAM participants in relevant schools); document analysis for SAM teams; and observations of inquiry team meetings.

2. The metric and scoring system was developed by New Visions for Public Schools to help its schools monitor student progress and intervene. New Visions provided us with student-level data for each graduation cohort in its approximately eighty schools, including eighth grade state test scores and demographics and on/off track status in 2011.

3. For details see Joan E. Talbert, with M. Ken Cor, Pai-rou Chen, Lambrina Mileva Kless, and Milbrey McLaughlin, *Inquiry-Based School Reform: Lessons from SAM in New York City* (Stanford, CA: Center for Research on the Context of Teaching, 2011), 14.

Chapter 3

1. Hereafter, our use of first names only indicate the use of pseudonyms.

2. The facilitator at New Dorp High School was Nell Scharff Panero. We give her the pseudonym Natasha not to conceal this fact but to emphasize that it is the role we feature rather than a specific facilitator.

3. In "From Looking at Scores to Understanding Student Thinking" (http://www.ascd.org/ascd-express/vol1/120-lineweaver.aspx), Lisa Lineweaver, Kristan Singleton, and Ellen Guiney point to language clues that signal missed opportunities for mining assessment data for information that will improve learning. Changed teacher language, they maintain, signals the desired shift in mind-set from "looking at scores" to "understanding student thinking."

4. The meaning of information displayed in a tennis chart cannot be understood separately from the assessments used to denote "mastery." Figure 3.3, for example, raises questions that should prompt a team to examine its assessments in order to become increasingly clear on what exactly target students can and cannot do. To understand figure 3.3, teachers need to analyze the questions on their assessment to determine whether or not the students do not know how to use *so*, whether they do not know the content involved and therefore did not apply *so* appropriately, and/or whether the question itself was problematic.

Chapter 4

1. In 1936, Maxie Woodring, of Teachers College, Columbia University, compared the need for teachers to closely examine their practice to the professional development of a master musician, whose success is the result of "hours upon hours of meticulous practice in minutely analyzed skills." "Teaching," she wrote, in promoting stenographic reports of lessons to improve instruction, "is the most highly skilled of all the professions, demanding . . . an ability to see and to appreciate the causative effects of small details on the master product." In building her argument, Woodring contributed to a research base that introduced stenographic reports as a supervisory tool, evaluated the impact on student outcomes of simply placing these reports in teachers' hands, and analyzed transcripts made from tape recordings to report patterns of teacher-talk and questioning across classrooms over time. See Maxie N. Woodring, "The Use of the Stenographic Lesson in Improving Instruction," *Teachers College Record* 37 (1936): 504–517 (quote on 504–505); Romiett Stevens, "Stenographic Reports of High School Lessons," *Teachers College Record* 11 (1910): 1–66; Walter D. Cocking, *Peabody Journal of Education* 8 (1930): 131–139; and James Hoetker and William P. Ahlbrand Jr., *American Educational Research Journal* 6 (1969): 145–167. This line of research culminated in three distinct, current evolutions: "script-taping," advocated by Madeline Hunter; "literal notes," associated with Jonathan Saphier and Research for Better Teaching; and low-inference transcriptions, used heavily and refined in the SAM certification program and used in strategic inquiry. Script-taping, literal notes, and LITs are all produced by the observer with the hope that refining one's ability to capture classroom discourse accurately and fluently will increase one's ability to *see* classrooms more completely and with subtlety, as compared to stenographic reports produced by a professional stenographer in order that they be objective. In each, the process is explicitly intended to help observers learn to distinguish objectively reported facts from judgment, skills they will need as supervisors. Script-taping and literal notes differ from LITs in that they leave interpretive power primarily in the hands of the observer. Script-tapers use a personal short-hand, portions of which they select to decode; literal-notes capture only those segments of a lesson that the observer deems most relevant. In contrast, the LIT documents an entire lesson so that relevant details can be identified and interpreted in multiple ways by two or more educators. See Madeline Hunter and Doug Russell, *Mastering Coaching and Supervision* (Thousand Oaks, CA: Corwin Press, 1989), 13–19; and Research for Better Teaching, Inc., www.rbteach.com.

2. For another description of this example, see Helen A. Scharff, Deirdre A. DeAngelis, and Joan E. Talbert, "Starting Small for Big School Improvement," *Principal Leadership* 10, no. 8 (2010): 58–61.

Chapter 5

1. These numbers exclude long-term absences.

2. The Quality Review Rating is a NYC tool to measure data-driven decision making schoolwide; "well-developed" is the highest possible rating.

3. For a description of this process at New Dorp, see Peg Tyre, "The Writing Revolution," *Atlantic Monthly,* October 2012, as well as her follow-up piece and response to the debate caused by the article: http://www.theatlantic.com/magazine/archive/2012/10/the-writing-revolution/309090/; http://www.theatlantic.com/national/archive/2012/10/the-author-of-the-writing-revolution-responds-to-the-debate/263799/; http://www.theatlantic.com/magazine/archive/2012/10/the-writing-revolution/309090/. The primary-source material on which New Dorp's program is based is available in Judith C. Hochman, *Teaching Basic Writing Skills: Strategies for Effective Expository Writing* (Longmount, CO: Sopris West, 2009).

4. Tyre's "The Writing Revolution" provides a detailed example of how sentence-improvement strategies develop oral language and class discussion.

5. Our description of Blackstone leaders' strategies and challenges and quotations are from Lisa Lineweaver, "SAM Goes Schoolwide: SAM Principles + RTI Framework = School-Wide Improvement" (paper, American Education Research Association, April 2011, New Orleans). Refinements are based on e-mail communications and personal correspondence with Lineweaver in 2012–2013.

6. This may be due to the fact that in the certification program small schools typically sent one team to represent the faculty, whereas large schools generally sent multiple teams. Although the proportions may be the same, the decision for a principal to send multiple teams (especially in the case of Hillcrest and New Dorp, both of which sent large numbers of teachers to be trained) likely reflects the school's investment in strategic inquiry as a primary strategy for schoolwide improvement. The same would not necessarily be the case for a principal of a small school sending one team.

Part III

1. Evidence comes from more than six years of research on strategic inquiry in New York City (2006–2012); five years of research on the Bay Area Research Collaborative's inquiry-based district reform initiative (2001–2006); two years of research on a professional learning community initiative in Austin, TX; and four years of research on district reform in Sanger, CA. Case studies of the Long Beach, CA, district include: Elizabeth Woody, Soung Bae, Sandra Park, and Jennifer Russell, "Long Beach Unified School District: Data-Driven Decision-Making to Improve High School Achievement," in *Snapshots of Reform: Districts Efforts to Raise Student Achievement across Diverse Communities in California* (Berkeley: Policy Analysis for California Education), 23–30; and James E. Austin, Allen S Grossman, Robert B. Schwartz, and Jennifer M. Suesse, *Managing at Scale in Long Beach Unified School District* (Cambridge, MA: Public Education Leadership Project at Harvard University, 2006). Research in New York City and the Bay Area was conducted by Talbert and colleagues in the Stanford University Center for Research on the Context of Teaching; research

in Austin and Sanger was conducted by Talbert and Jane L. David of the Bay Area Research Group. Research reports for each project are available on the Stanford CRC Education Web site (http://www.stanford.edu/group/suse-crc/cgi-bin/drupal/).

Chapter 6

1. For further information, visit the Web site "All Things PLC" (http://www.allthingsplc.inf), built and maintained by the organization Solution Tree.

2. For analysis of how collaborative inquiry complements other strands of New York City's reform during the Bloomberg-Klein years, see Jennifer A. O'Day, Catherine S. Bitter, and Louis M. Gomez, eds., *Education Reform in New York City: Ambitious Change in the Nation's Most Complex School System* (Cambridge, MA: Harvard Education Press, 2011).

3. For further discussion, see Jane L. David and Joan E. Talbert, *Turning Around a High-Poverty School District: Learning from Sanger Unified's Success* (Palo Alto, CA: Bay Area Research Group; Stanford, CA: Center for Research on the Context of Teaching, 2012).

4. The description is based on Woody, Bae, Park, and Russell, "Long Beach Unified School District," 23–30; David and Talbert, "Turning Around a High-Poverty School District;" and Richard DuFour, Rebecca DuFour, Robert Eaker, and Gayle Karhanek, "Under No Circumstances Blame the Kids: Sanger Unified School District," *Raising the Bar and Closing the Gap: Whatever It Takes* (Bloomington, IN: Solution Tree, 2006).

5. Woody, Bae, Park, and Russell, "Long Beach Unified School District," 27.

6. Research suggests that significant shifts in school culture take about three years of sustained effort. The estimate of five years for district reform assumes a two-year period for creating sufficient numbers of well-trained strategic inquiry facilitators to support teacher teams in all district schools. Depending on district size, this time period might be shortened or lengthened by a year.

7. New York City developed an evolving set of online tools and resources to support its Collaborative Inquiry initiative over the first few years. See Joan E. Talbert, "Collaborative Inquiry to Expand Student Success in New York City Schools," in O'Day, Bitter, and Gomez, *Education Reform in New York City.*

8. Organizational theory contrasts bureaucratic and professional modes of authority and controls as fundamentally opposed modes of organizing work. The former controls work through hierarchy, rules, and sanctions and the latter through professional standards, expertise, and mutual accountability. Dan Lortie's classic study *Schoolteacher: A Sociological Study* (Chicago: University of Chicago Press, 1975) applied the distinction to education, warning that the growth of educational bureaucracies was a threat to teacher professionalism.

   For further discussion, see Joan E. Talbert, "Professional Learning Communities at the Crossroads: How Systems Hinder or Engender Change," *International Handbook of Educational Change, Vol. 2* (Springer Press, 2010).

9. Austin, Grossman, Schwartz, and Suesse, *Managing at Scale in Long Beach Unified School District*, 8.

10. Ibid., 7.

11. David and Talbert, *Turning Around a High-Poverty School District*, 48.

Chapter 7

1. See Arthur Levine's condemnation of existing programs in *Educating School Leaders*, The Education Schools Project, 2005, http://www.edschools.org/pdf/Final313.pdf. Also see Lee Mitgang's report *The Making of a Principal: Five Lessons in Leadership Training* (New York: Wallace Foundation, 2012), which states: "All too often, training has failed to keep pace with the evolving role of principals. This is especially true at most of the 500-plus university-based programs where the majority of school leaders are trained" (6). This report quotes Michelle Young, executive director of the University Council for Educational Administration, who states that in 1987 the National Committee on Excellence in Educational Administration recommended that 250 of the 500 existing programs be closed. When asked what proportion currently has quality, she said, "I'd say that out of that 500 you've got about 200 that are pretty solid" (15).

2. Successful models of district-university partnerships to promote inquiry-based improvement include Sanger Unified School District's partnership with Fresno State University to provide some onsite classes led by district experts and focused on the district's inquiry-based reform leadership model and Long Beach Unified's close partnership with Cal State Long Beach to prepare both teachers and administrators for a collaborative inquiry district culture. For a description of how eight districts demonstrate their power to "grab . . . program attention and demand better 'products,' thereby stimulating better training," see *Knowledge in Brief: When Urban School Districts Demand It, Principal Training and Preparation Can Improve*, Wallace Foundation, October 2010, http://www.wallacefoundation.org/knowledge-center/school-leadership/key-research/Documents/Districts-Developing-Leaders-Key-findings-from-wallace.pdf; and Margaret T. Orr, Cheryl King, and Michelle La Pointe, *Districts Developing Leaders: Lessons on Consumer Actions and Program Approaches from Eight Urban Districts* (New York: Educational Development Center, 2010).

3. From here on we refer to instructors in SAM as *facilitators* to emphasize that their role is essentially the same as in the noncertification version of strategic inquiry and to suggest some key differences in the role from that of a typical university instructor.

4. For a description of the ALPS program, see Sandra J. Stein and Liz Gewirtzman, *Principal Training on the Ground: Ensuring Highly Qualified School Leadership* (Portsmouth, NH: Heinemann, 2003).

5. For evidence that subject departments traditionally are the locus of decision making and leadership in high schools, see, for example, Leslie S. Siskin, *Realms of Knowledge:*

Academic Departments in Secondary Schools (London: Falmer Press, 1994), and Milbrey W. McLaughlin and Joan E. Talbert, *Professional Communities and the Work of High School Teaching* (Chicago: University of Chicago Press, 2001).

6. In 2002 Constancia Warren of the Carnegie Corporation of New York observed Sandra Stein teaching in ALPS, liked what she saw, and asked Stein to design an administrator preparation program like ALPS specifically for high schools. This task then fell to Gewirtzman, who came on board full-time at Baruch when Stein was recruited as academic dean for the newly formed New York City Leadership Academy.

7. SAM I schools were Hillcrest, Bayard Rustin, the Bronx Guild, and Humanities Prep. The program was funded by the Carnegie Corporation of New York, and the grant sat at Baruch College on behalf of the Baruch/New Visions partnership. Curriculum was adapted from ALPS by SAM leaders in conversation with SAM I principals John Angelet, Vince Brevetti, Stephen Duch, Michael Soguero, and others, including Anthony Connelli, Sandy Ferguson, Sandra Stein, and Shael Polakow-Suransky.

8. The New York City Leadership Academy, an independent nonprofit, was launched in 2003 specifically to prepare principals for New York City public schools. With Sandra Stein as its first academic dean, its curriculum, pedagogical approach, and core ideas drew heavily on those of ALPS, which she, Liz Gewirtzman, and district partners had codeveloped at Baruch. Key differences included a more integrated curriculum with a cohort taught by one facilitator over time (an ALPS cohort moved through discrete courses); more elaborate simulations (ALPs was more problem-based); summer intensives; and a year-long residency intended as a practice field. SAM was launched with a simulation-based summer intensive and an integrated curriculum taught by a consistent facilitator from the start but diverged from the Leadership Academy in that the residency could be more fully integrated over the entire course of the program, since participating teams worked on their actual schools' improvement throughout. Over time, the purposes and expertise of the Leadership Academy and SAM diverged: the first focused primarily on preparing and supporting new principals and the second on school improvement through the leadership development of teams. Both became increasingly focused on evidence-based decision making and improvement in parallel with the Klein administration's approach.

9. New Visions schools in SAM III (over four iterations) were funded by a grant from the Carnegie Corporation of New York. This grant sat at New Visions on behalf of the Baruch/New Visions partnership. For iterations II–IV, New Visions provided facilitators and recruited and interfaced with participating schools. Baruch provided curriculum and facilitator training. For iteration II, Liz Gewirtzman served as program director and Nell Scharff Panero as lead facilitator. In iterations III and IV, Gewirtzman led SAM nationally (supporting SAM in Oakland, Boston, and Rochester), and Panero became director of SAM in New York City. Schools from another NYC network also sent teams to iterations II–IV. These cohorts were funded solely through student tuition. Their facilitator, Isora Bailey, was paid by the district since she facilitated their learning in SAM as her method of district support.

10. The weekly facilitator meetings were the main forum for surfacing challenges and deriving lessons through practice, which then translated into decisions about design changes. Through these weekly meetings, SAM designers better understood what aspects of program design were not clearly articulated. Facilitators and designers worked together to better articulate the role of systems from the start and to ensure that foregrounding systems was reflected in revised assignments.

11. SAM Citywide was created to provide greater access to the SAM certification program for those ineligible to apply because of the team requirement. The curriculum was developed through a New York State/Wallace Foundation grant in collaboration with Brooklyn College, Lehman College, the New York City Leadership Academy, and the New York City Department of Education, for which Liz Gewirtzman was the principal investigator, and it is implemented with the cooperation of New Visions for Public Schools.

12. See Rosa Rivera-McCutchen and Nell Scharff, "Leading Peer Coaching for School Improvement" (paper, American Educational Research Association, New Orleans, April 2011).

13. Joan E. Talbert, with M. Ken Cor, Pai-rou Chen, Lambrina Mileva Kless, and Milbrey McLaughlin, *Inquiry-Based School Reform: Lessons from SAM in NYC* (Palo Alto, CA: Center for Research on the Context of Teaching, 2012).

14. For an example of an aligned certification-bearing leadership program, see Collaborative Leadership Advancing Student and School Success (CLASS), designed and run through a collaboration of Hunter College, City University of New York, and New Visions for Public Schools. The program launched in January 2013 with a curriculum drawing heavily on SAM.

15. This discussion assumes that teams are not already commonplace in the district. If they are, a program might choose to accept individual participants who are on school teams, as in SAM Citywide.

16. ISLLC standards were developed by the Council of Chief State School Officers and test knowledge, dispositions, and skills in the following six domains: vision and evidence-based continuous improvement; culture and the instructional environment; management of operations and resources; families and communities; ethics and reflective practice; and advocacy. See http://coe.fgcu.edu/faculty/valesky/isllcstandards.htm.

Acknowledgments

We are deeply grateful to the New York City school and district leaders who opened their doors and practices to us as we facilitated and evaluated strategic inquiry over nearly a decade. Our book rests on their dedication and persistent hard work to improve student success. Their and their students' experiences and voices are at the core of this book and ground our understandings of what it takes to change schools into learning organizations that make steady gains in student achievement.

We thank the Carnegie Corporation of New York, especially Constancia Warren, for soliciting and supporting an experimental design in leadership preparation for high schools, and Michele Cahill, for sustaining this investment in the leader credentialing program that spawned strategic inquiry and its evaluation to develop knowledge for the field.

Thanks go to the organizations that partnered to make the work happen: the School of Public Affairs at Baruch College, City University of New York, and New Visions for Public Schools. At Baruch, we are especially grateful to Liz Gewirtzman, the primary founder of SAM. More than anyone else, she is the thinker at the heart of the program. Her insistence on open source and the collaborative pushing of ideas to always become better set the standard and has allowed strategic inquiry to thrive. At Baruch, we also thank Stan Altman, David Birdsell, Jonathan Engel, Michael Lovaglio, Maureen Samedy, Angelina Delgado, and Melissa Sultana. At New Visions for Public Schools, we are especially grateful to Robert Hughes, Ron Chaluisan, Stacy Martin, Beverly Donohue, Deb Goss, Carl Watson, Chad Vignola, and Joan Walrond for their proactive partnership and steadfast support.

We gratefully acknowledge the contributions of roughly fifty principals and three hundred participants in all New York City SAM teams for their commitment to strategic inquiry, hard work implementing it, and contributions to program refinements over the years. Special thanks go to the twelve schools that participated in the evaluation's longitudinal case studies. We are especially indebted to two superstar principals, Deirdre DeAngelis and Stephen Duch, whose leadership of strategic inquiry and stunning school success is featured in this book and because of whom the model has taken its current shape. From you and the work of administrators, teachers, and students at your schools we have learned more than we can say.

We thank the SAM facilitators for their innumerable contributions to the ideas and evidence that ground strategic inquiry. We are especially grateful to Isora Bailey, Susie Greenebaum, Felicia Hirata, Rosa Rivera-McCutchen, Lisa Lineweaver, and Michelle Brochu—each of whom has facilitated multiple iterations of the model and played a critical role in the design and tools presented here. We also thank John Angelet, Vince Breveti, Stephen Duch, and Michael Soguero (principals/cofacilitators in the SAM pilot), as well as Alisa Berger, Lydell Carter, Mark Dunetz, Jennifer Goldstein, Brad Haggerty, Dan Scanlon, Stephanie Sibley, Kathleen Smith, Emily White, Ann Wiener, and Sandy Yark (facilitators of subsequent iterations). We thank Judith Hochman, whose strategies for teaching expository writing brought improvement through inquiry to the next level and form a critical element of the New Dorp story. To those thanked here, we've barely scratched the surface of our collective inquiry and hope you think this book does justice to what we have learned together so far.

We also thank colleagues at Stanford's Center for Research on the Context of Teaching for their many contributions to the evaluation of strategic inquiry in New York City schools. Milbrey McLaughlin and Lambrina Mileva Kress collaborated on the design and analysis of multiyear case studies of schools with and without teams participating in the SAM program. Wendy Lin and Ken Cor developed longitudinal survey and student achievement data bases and carried out quantitative analysis of school change. Special thanks to Cor for conducting the matched-sample analysis of student outcomes and to Pai-rou Chen for managing our complex, multimethod database over the years. Thanks also to our

New York City colleague John Schoener for help with data collection. Finally, we acknowledge and thank Jane L. David of the Bay Area Research Group for her collaboration with Talbert on several studies beyond New York City that inform our analysis of the district role in inquiry-based school reform.

Last but not least, we thank Harvard Education Press editor Carolyn Chauncey for her support from start to finish. Her enthusiasm and suggestions at each stage of the book's conception and execution have been invaluable. She's been a wonderful steward and colleague, and we are deeply grateful.

About the Authors

Nell Scharff Panero is the director of the Center for Educational Leadership (CEL) in the School of Public Affairs at Baruch College, City University of New York. In 2004 she joined Baruch to teach in the Aspiring Leaders Program. Since 2005 she has codeveloped, taught in, trained trainers in, and refined (with Liz Gewirtzman) the Scaffolded Apprenticeship Model (SAM) of school improvement through leadership development. As a consultant, she has established inquiry as an engine of improvement in multiple large high schools and helped schools, districts, and universities to adapt and apply the model in both certification and noncertification versions. Her research interests include inquiry-based continuous improvement and facilitator development. Currently she runs the latest SAM iteration at Baruch (SAM Citywide) and, under the auspices of CEL, promotes broad knowledge and understanding of effective writing instruction—in particular, of strategies that were proven to close pervasive skill gaps surfaced through strategic inquiry. She holds a bachelor's degree in English from Kenyon College, a master's in English from Hunter College, and a doctorate in English education from New York University. Prior to teaching at Baruch, she taught English at Hunter College High School for thirteen years. Her previous publications include the *Children First Intensive Inquiry Team Handbook* (New York City Department of Education, 2008) and "Starting Small for Big School Improvement," *Principal Leadership* (April 2010, with D. A. DeAngelis and J. E. Talbert).

Joan E. Talbert is Senior Research Scholar Emerita in Stanford University's School of Education. She joined the faculty in 1977 and cofounded (with Milbrey McLaughlin) the Center for Research on the Context of

Teaching (CRC) in 1987 through a U.S. Department of Education Center grant. She was a member-at-large of the American Education Research Association Council and the National Research Council's Committee on Education Finance. She holds a bachelor's degree in sociology from Vassar College and a master's degree and doctorate in sociology from the University of Washington. With CRC colleagues, she investigates conditions that shape teaching and learning, especially school-based professional communities. Through more than a dozen multiyear studies in school districts across the country, she has documented the results of various approaches to fostering teacher learning communities that continuously improve student achievement. Currently she is studying successful district reform strategies in the Central Valley of California. Her previous books include *Building School-Based Teacher Learning Communities in Schools: Professional Strategies to Improve Student Achievement,* coauthored with M. W. McLaughlin (Teachers College Press, 2006), and *Professional Communities and the Work of High School Teaching,* coauthored with M. W. McLaughlin (University of Chicago Press, 2001). Her recent book chapters and articles include "Collaborative Inquiry to Expand Student Achievement in New York City Schools," in *Education Reform in New York City: Ambitious Change in the Nation's Most Complex School System,* ed. J. O'Day, C. Bitter, and J. Gomez (Harvard Education Press, 2011); "Professional Learning Communities at the Crossroads: How Systems Hinder or Engender Change," *International Handbook of Educational Change,* vol. 2 (Springer Press, 2010); "Conceptions of Evidence Use in School Districts: Mapping the Terrain," coauthored with C. E. Coburn, *American Journal of Education* (August 2006).

Index